AN EXTRA-TERRESTRIAL AND PARANORMAL HISTORY

TIMELESS
TRINITY

by Bruce Olav Solheim, Ph.D. • Illustrations by Gary Dumm
Foreword by Yvonne Smith, CHT

Timeless Trinity:
An Extra-Terrestrial and Paranormal Personal History

By Bruce Olav Solheim, Ph.D.
Illustrations by Gary Dumm

Edited by George Verongos

Copyright © 2020 Bruce Olav Solheim

ISBN: 978-0-578-62745-8

Boots to Books
Glendora, CA 91741 USA
bootstobooks@gmail.com
www.bruceolavsolheim.com

Acknowledgements

The list of people who have been instrumental in supporting me in writing this *Timeless* trilogy continues to grow. I'm indebted to Esther Jenkins, Terry Lovelace, Dr. Edwin M. Young, Dr. Dean Radin, the folks in the Citrus College Continuing Education office, the Citrus College custodial staff, Dr. Dana Hester, Dr. Eric Rabitoy, Heather Heselton, Sheena Metal, Mickey Mikkelson with Creative Edge Publicity, Dr. Dale Salwak, Terje Simonsen, David Willson, my paranormal students, Dr. Simeon Hein, Dr. Jeffrey Mishlove, Yvonne Smith, James Lough, Lucinda Morel, Dr. Michael Masters, George Noory, Diane Eaton, Jo Wood, Dave Schrader, Louie B. Free, Robert Sharpe, Christie Stratos, Lyn Buchanan, Victoria at Contact in the Desert, Whitley Strieber, Bob Lazar, Philip Corso, Kathleen Marden, Travis Walton, and many others I may have forgotten. The foundation upon which all my work rests was provided by my parents, my Norwegian ancestors, and my immediate family: Ginger, Leif, Caitlin, Bjørn, Byron, Mary, Courtney, and my grandchildren. I would like to thank my special friends Gene Thorkildsen, and Maia. The creative talents of Gary and Laura Dumm, and George Verongos have taken my vision to heights I could only imagine at the beginning. I would also like to thank Anzar, Ergot, Theodora, Ozzie, Archangel Michael, Jesus, and God. I'm a work in progress, as are we all.

Just as a reminder to my readers, the stories in this book reflect my recollection of events. Some names, locations, and identifying characteristics have been changed to protect the privacy of those depicted. Dialogue has been re-created from memory.

Foreword

In early 2019, I received an email from Bruce Olav Solheim, Ph.D. who was seeking help about an unsettling memory he had back when he was nineteen years old. He consciously recalls seeing a column of fire in front of him and feeling paralyzed while hearing a strange voice that absolutely terrified him. Bruce is a well-respected professor at Citrus College in the Southern California area. He enjoys teaching his U.S. History classes and his students greatly admire him. I had the privilege of lecturing for his Paranormal Personal History Class where I met his students who were very interested in the UFO/Abduction phenomena. He and his wife, Ginger, live in an upper middle-class neighborhood and enjoy a "normal" life. Bruce's profile is representative of hundreds of thousands of Experiencers. Ordinary people living with an extraordinary secret. It is from these unsung heroes where the deepest revelations of the phenomenon are coming from, and it's time we hear their stories with a compassionate ear. Some faction of our United States government still chooses to deny the fact that nonhuman intelligences are engaging with its citizens, despite the evidence being overwhelming. So much so, it would stand in a court of law. The lid on Pandora's Box can only be kept on for so long. Even our Navy and their skilled pilots have come forward with the now-famous USS Nimitz event, as highlighted in the following excerpt from a Live Science article from January 2020:

In November 2004, several U.S. Navy pilots stationed aboard the USS Nimitz encountered a Tic-Tac-shaped UFO darting and dashing over the Pacific Ocean in apparent defiance of the laws of physics. Navy officials dubbed the strange craft an "unidentified aerial phenomenon," but they have remained mum on what, exactly, that phenomenon could've been. Now, unsurprisingly to anyone who's ever considered making a hat out of tinfoil, the military has confirmed they know more than they're letting on. In response to a recent Freedom of Information Act (FOIA) request, a spokesperson from the Navy's Office of Naval Intelligence (ONI) confirmed that the agency possesses several top-secret documents and at least one classified video pertaining to the 2004 UFO encounter.

During the 2019 International UFO Congress, I spoke with Kevin Day, one of the radar operators who observed the Tic-Tac UFO, who was kind enough to give me a copy of his book, *Sailor's Anthology*. The chapter "The See'r" is a fictionalized account of the Nimitz encounter. He felt the need to shroud his experience in the veil of fiction out of fear of ridicule and to protect the identities of colleagues. "After retiring from the United States Navy," he writes, "memories of the encounter continued to trouble me greatly. When I did try to tell others my story, I could tell that nobody really believed me, or they believed there had to be a more prosaic explanation." For those who make the decision to come forward to speak about their lifelong experiences publicly, they have more to lose than to gain. These brave souls do so not for money or fame (since the money is non-existent and they become "infamous" as opposed to famous). They choose to reach out to those people who feel alone and vulnerable so they can understand what is happening to them. I am hoping, with the dawn of a new decade, those with the burden of extraordinary encounters no longer have to hide. I have been working with abduction cases for the last twenty-nine years, and a year after I started my practice and research, I founded the support group CERO (Close Encounter Resource Organization). After working intimately in private sessions with individuals who have had lifelong experiences, I began to see how isolated they all felt after they left my office. I am often the first person someone confides in with their lifelong secret. Isolation, the fear of ridicule, the fear of being placed in a psychiatric hospital are all common among Abductees. They tell me they hope to be diagnosed as "crazy" so they can take a pill and it will all go away. This is a very sad commentary about a phenomenon that is all too real. When receiving Bruce's answers to my routine questionnaire, he presented as having difficulty sleeping, depression, anxiety, hyper vigilance, flashback memories, nightmares and having difficulty maintaining close relationships. Like so many hundreds of people who have contacted me over the years in hopes of making sense of their sketchy memories, Bruce felt a need to begin his journey of exploration after many years of wondering and questioning himself. Bruce's journey began on April 6, 2019. His hypnotic regression sessions have painted a clearer picture of the half memories he has had since childhood. In this book, Bruce eloquently takes the reader through his regression and formulates his own conclusions about what it all means to him. *Timeless Trinity: An Extra Terrestrial and Paranormal Personal History* serves as a go-to for those who are beginning to awaken to the meaning of their half memories and PTSD symptoms. I thank Bruce for his trust and confidence in my work as his Hypnotherapist and I admire his courage to speak openly and live his truth.

Yvonne R. Smith, C.Ht.
Los Angeles, California
January 2020

Table of Contents

Prologue: Give Me Liberty or Give Me Death

Several months ago, I was switching my medical treatment and care to the Long Beach Veterans Administration (VA) Medical Center. As the intake nurse was looking over a survey I had filled out, she asked if I ever heard voices from people who weren't really there or seen people that weren't there. I laughed and said, "I didn't mark yes on your sheet, but I have psychic-mediumship abilities, so I can tell you that I do hear them, I do see them, and they're really there." She smiled nervously.

Dr. Solheim has been abducted by aliens several times and talks to dead people on a regular basis. That sounds like the beginning of a competency hearing that wouldn't go well for me. The truth is the truth, no matter how uncomfortable it may be. I want to know the truth, and I suspect so does everyone else. So, what is it that stops us from pursuing the truth about the paranormal? Answer: Fear. I, for one, am tired of living in fear. We must liberate ourselves from the conventions and constraints of the past and adopt a bold new vision. As American patriot Patrick Henry wrote in 1775, "I know not what course others may take; as for me, give me liberty or give me death."

"His problem is that he doesn't know his place." That is what a senior college administrator once said about me at an academic dean's meeting. One of the deans in attendance told me this later in confidence. I suppose it was meant to be mean, but it sounded more like frustration on his part. I had gone over his head and that of my dean to talk directly to the college president and start a unique distance education program for the US Navy that proved to be very successful. I consider his statement to be a great compliment. I'm glad that I have the freedom not to know my place. Where would this country be if everyone stayed in their

1

place and tacitly accepted what others told them or expected of them? None of our American heroes were such timid creatures. President Barack Obama wrote a book entitled: *The Audacity of Hope*. I believe not only in the audacity of hope but in the audacity of purpose and action. As Georges Danton, a leader in the early stages of the French Revolution, wrote in 1792: *"L'audace, l'audace, toujours l'audace."* Or, in English, "Audacity, audacity, always audacity."

Although I'm no hero, I'll admit that it was risky for me as an academic to publish paranormal books. I suppose critics could say that my first *Timeless* book was the work of an eccentric professor nearing retirement. *Timeless Deja Vu*, on the other hand, might have given them a reason for concern, while this third book, may prove that I'm certifiable and should be locked up or silenced through some kind of academic *fatwa*. Just kidding. I don't worry about the critics; I publish what I'm compelled to publish, and if the people like it and it helps them in some small way, so much the better. It's unbelievable how successful the other books have been not to mention my paranormal personal history class, which is now being offered twice a year. My radio show, *Timeless Esoterica*, is doing well and we've had many intriguing guests covering a wide range of topics. I've been interviewed on *Coast to Coast AM* and many other radio programs. I hope that someday my *Timeless* trilogy will be translated into other languages. None of this would mean anything if it were not for the fact that we're helping people. My message is simple: Live forever and be the light. There is no reason to fear death because we're timeless, and love is the most important force in the universe, and it's forever.

I've come to embrace having psychic medium abilities fully. One of the first things I learned was that it's not about being right or wrong; it's about helping—that is the first rule of mediumship. You can't let your ego get in the way. I'm not

2

special or better than anyone else; I'm just me. You must maintain humble confidence, which is no easy task for us mere mortals who tend to gravitate back and forth from conceit to calamity. In other words, I have a gift but it's not about me; it's about the spirits and their loved ones. *Timeless Trinity* is aptly named because it's the most spiritual book in the *Timeless* trilogy, referring to the Christian Godhead, and explores the three realities postulated by physicist David Bohm. In addition to my paranormal personal history, I'll offer you, dear reader, direct communication that I've received from the spirit world and from extra-terrestrials that may be of some comfort.

Dr. Dean Radin, Chief Scientist at the Institute of Noetic Sciences, wrote in *Real Magic* that: "The essence of magic boils down to the application of two ordinary mental skills: attention and intention. The strength of the magical outcome is modulated by four factors: belief, imagination, emotion, and clarity. That's basically it. The ceremonial robes, somber settings, black candles, secret handshakes, chanting in ancient languages, sex, and drugs—all are good theater, which may help in withdrawing the mind from the distractions of the mundane world. But ultimately, they're unnecessary." I agree with sticking to the basics because the paranormal is quite normal, and the supernatural is quite natural. This brings me back to the point that I made before, in *Timeless Deja Vu,* quoting my departed friend Gene Thorkildsen, "Experiencing is believing and believing is experiencing." For a person who hasn't experienced, or better said, hasn't acknowledged a paranormal event in their life, it's easy to dismiss any notion of such strange things. However, not wanting something to be true, when it's true, doesn't make it go away, no matter how hard you try.

When I was a young child, I often thought that maybe I'm living another life and that I had already died. In other words, reincarnation. Nobody taught me that. I felt it and thought it. I liked hanging out in graveyards. Nobody instructed me to do that. It was my own idea. This is just one of many of my childhood beliefs that have been validated and have played out. In my first two *Timeless* books, I discussed my childhood belief that we all lived in the belly of a giant. I think that conception helped me understand the interconnectedness and wonder of the universe. I've always allowed my imagination to guide me in exploring consciousness. My occasional startling sense of self-awareness is a reminder that I'm alive and connected to everything, all the time.

The stories in this third *Timeless* book delve deeper into the paranormal and take you, dear reader, into brave new worlds of adventure and understanding. I deal more directly with alien life, for instance (one look at the cover and you know). It's my understanding that we've been visited by aliens since the beginning of humankind. Alien activity has accelerated lately, and I'm not the only one to have noticed this. I realize that some folks might grudgingly accept that ghosts may indeed exist, or that telepathy is real, but they draw the line when it comes to aliens. It reminds me of the old trick played by intelligence agencies when they're covering up their actions: don't attack the message, attack the messenger. In other words, aren't all people who have claimed to have seen UFOs or told stories of alien abduction crazy? You know, tinfoil hats and all? The simple answer is no, these people aren't crazy, they're telling the truth, and the truth has been covered up. I'm one of those people and belong to a group of other fearless, brave souls who have stepped forward. The group is known as CERO: Close Encounters Research Organization.

As I wrote in *Timeless Deja Vu*, the process of disclosure reminds me of the words generally attributed to German philosopher Arthur Schopenhauer. To paraphrase: All truth passes through three stages. First, it is ridiculed. Second, it is violently opposed. Third, it is accepted as being self-evident. So, what is the connection between ghosts and aliens? Well, since the spirit world is the quantum world, it makes sense that advanced alien beings would know this and operate in that realm, meaning that the spirit world, the alien world, and the quantum world are actually one.

Dr. Edwin M. Young, a scientist who ran a psychic research lab at Stanford University in the 1970s, told me that matter vibrates constantly in and out of our reality. Matter is a condensed form of energy that is guided by mind focus and powered by spirit. I'm not a scientist, but this pretty much sounds like the unified theory of everything that scientists have been looking for. Could it be that we simply create our own realities? Affirmative. As children, we hadn't yet learned the laws and social customs we were to obey. We observed everything around us without preconception and judgment. As we started school and learned society's acceptable "truths," our youthful, unfettered view of the world was channeled and shaped into acceptable ways of thinking. For instance, I had two "make-believe" playmates, John and Johnny. To me, as a young boy, they were real, as was my teddy bear and other stuffed animals. I also talked to animals, especially our cats. Slowly, I was convinced that they weren't real and couldn't speak and that if I persisted in acting as if they were communicating with me, people would think I was crazy and shun me and lock me away. Luckily, I pretended to follow society's conventions but secretly held on to my childhood experiences and beliefs. That has made all the difference in my life.

This book reaches further than the first two *Timeless* books. In so doing, I've taken more risks, and dared to present subjects that most academics would run from in horror, for to write about them, is to "commit academic suicide" as one graduate student said. I believe in living life boldly and taking risks when the need arises and is justified. As Alfred, Lord Tennyson, wrote in his epic poem, *The Charge of the Light Brigade:*

Forward the Light Brigade!
Was there a man dismay'd?
Not tho' the soldier knew
Some one had blunder'd:
Theirs not to make reply,
Theirs not to reason why,
Theirs but to do & die,
Into the valley of Death
Rode the six hundred.

When Patrick Henry said: "Give me liberty or give me death," he wasn't kidding around. What is this life worth living for if you're not living it free and truthfully? As my spirit guides so often tell me: "Stay in the light, feel the light, be the light." So, my friends, it's okay to be different, to think differently, and to live your own true, authentic life as you sense it in every possible way. To do otherwise is not to be honest. As we grow older, we come to realize that we're all the heroes of our own life story and truly embrace the full meaning of Shakespeare's words, "to thine own self be true." Indeed, it comes down to this, I really don't know my place, and neither should you.

Big Bad John (1964)

Now I lay me down to sleep.
I pray the Lord my soul to keep.
If I should die before I wake,
I pray the Lord my soul to take. Amen.

Not only is this part of the break in the Metallica song "Enter Sandman," but it's also the prayer I said every night when I was growing up, full of fear. No wonder I was afraid. I've always thought that it was a strange prayer for a little kid. I decided to explore these childhood fears through a hypnotic regression session with Yvonne Smith, the world-renowned hypnotherapist. You never know what you'll dig up under hypnosis. It usually begins with a question. When I was growing up in Kenmore, Washington, why did I fear to look out the window in my bedroom that faced our backyard? Could it be because my brother moved downstairs to his new room when I was six years old, and I was afraid to be alone in the room? He is nine years older than me, so I'm sure it was good for him to have his own room, but for the first time in my short life I had a room to myself, and I was frightened.

As a child, I was afraid of the dark, and there were many nights that I had nightmares and ended up in my parents' bed. In those days, our house had woods in the back and to the north. During the daytime, those woods were a dream come true for my friends and me, and we had lots of fun adventures exploring and imagining among the tall cedars and Douglas firs, western maple, and alder trees. At night, however, it was a dark, mysterious, and ominous place that we dared not venture out into, even on a double dare. After the sun went down, we imagined that there

7

were creatures out there that roamed those trails–ghosts, goblins, witches, zombies, vampires, werewolves, aliens, and many other things that terrified my little buddies and me. A few years ago, I returned to my old neighborhood and found that the woods were gone and were replaced by houses, everywhere, jammed together. All the current residents are strangers to me—not surprising because I moved away in 1978. Back to my fear of the dark and my scary window in my childhood bedroom, there is something hidden away in the dark recesses of my mind. I suspected that there was more to the story, and it required a hypnotic regression.

I remember being an odd little kid. I saw things differently than most of my buddies. For one thing, my relationship with the dead set me apart from my peers. I wrote about my desire to hang out in graveyards in my first *Timeless* book (see "Let's Do Lunch"). I liked to speak to adults and often made friends with them more easily than with other children. I also didn't mind playing by myself. I spent many hours playing with my Tonka trucks in the dirt in the backyard alongside my imaginal (more real than imaginary) playmates, playing army in the woods, or fantasizing about being in outer space. My imaginal playmates were John and Johnny. Some of you who read my previous books and stories may wonder if this is the same Johnny that was my neighborhood friend. That Johnny had a different name in real life—I changed it to Johnny for privacy reasons. Johnny, my "invisible" playmate, was a little kid like me. My other "invisible" playmate was John, or as I also called him, Big Bad John. He was grown up and not always very friendly. When I say invisible, I mean that they were invisible to other people, not to me; that is why the term imaginal is more appropriate. They were very real to me, and I did see them, talk to them, and play with them.

On one of my spirit walks, I asked my big sister Bjørg (who passed away in 2014) if she remembers what I was like as a child.

"You were unusual, that's true. You could carry on conversations with grown people easily," she said.

"Did I ever talk about flying?" I asked.

"Oh yeah, and spacemen. We thought it was because you watched science fiction movies and then later because of *Lost in Space* and *Star Trek*. You know, we thought it was just imagination," she said.

"How about imaginal playmates? You know, imaginary, invisible..."

"Yes, you had those, can't remember their names, but yes," she said. Then I decided to ask my mom, who resides in the spirit world since she passed away in 1990.

"Mom, what was I like as a child and growing up?"

"You had invisible friends. You were always building spaceships, playing with rockets, you had a Mercury lunchbox, and you liked the TV show *Lost in Space*. I bought you a flying saucer toy. You used to watch scary movies, and you talked to ghosts. There was one time when I walked into our recreation room, and you were watching a movie where aliens were drinking the blood of animals," Mom said.

"I remember that my stories scared you," I said.

"Yes, sometimes, when you were a young teenager, I used to come into your room to clean...very messy by the way...but you would have stories that you had written lying on your desk. I read them and got so scared I had to leave your room," she said.

"Sorry, Mom," I said. She smiled that knowing smile that she had.

I grew up near a Nike missile base in Kenmore. The facility, which was on the top of the hill above our house less than one-quarter of a mile away, was taken over by the Army National Guard in 1959 and was previously run by the regular Army from 1956 to 1959. The site, designated as S-03 (the S stood for Seattle Defense Area), became operational in 1956 and remained in service through 1964. The Nike site above our house was the control and administrative center; the actual missiles were kept in silos at a separate Nike site not far away. Today our Nike site is called Horizon Heights Park, and all the military structures have been removed. Over twenty years ago, I brought my daughter to play at the park and struck up conversations with other parents. None of them knew that the park used to be a Nike site. A few buildings survive at the launch site one mile away, now a Federal Emergency Management Agency (FEMA) regional headquarters and Army Reserve Center. We grew up with a constant flow of army trucks driving up 55th Avenue Northeast; in fact, my brother was hit by an army truck when he was little. The Army would never confirm or deny that the missiles were armed with nuclear weapons. But there was little doubt. Aliens and UFOs have been known to frequent military bases, especially those that have or control nuclear weapons.

What follows is from my June 8, 2019, and August 3, 2019, hypnotherapy sessions with Yvonne Smith. She asked me to go back in my mind and thoughts to my family home when I was six years old and describe what I see. I was able to return to that period of my life quickly under hypnosis.

"I'm in the hallway that leads back to my bedroom, that I used to share with my brother. My parents' room is off to the left, bathroom to the right. The light blue fixtures in the bathroom are inviting and nostalgic," I said. On the other side of the hallway is a closet with lots of shelves that I liked to explore. I remember there was an old hairdryer made from steel and wood, and a shoebox with odd things, like my dad's wedding ring that he had worn down to the point that it looked like a broken piece of wire. On another shelf, there was a 1950s-vintage portable record player.

Yvonne asked me to describe what I was wearing as I walked around.

"I'm wearing a striped shirt and brown pants, socks, no shoes," I said. I looked into mom and dad's room, and I saw their dark pink bedspread, it was shiny. The bookcase headboard was beige and had a few books and some reading glasses on the shelves. I then walked into my room at the end of the hallway.

"To the right is my bed, with the foot of the bed facing the window. I see my stuffed animals on the bed with a green bedspread with black and white stripes. My stuffed animals are my protectors—Teddy, Linus, Tiger, Weiner Dog, Squirrely," I said. The window had curtains, beige, with gold metal threads woven throughout. The window was higher up on the wall, but I could see out of it without standing on something. My cat liked to freak-out and jump on the curtains and claw them sometimes, which would make my mom mad.

"What do you see when you look out the window," asked Yvonne. I paused.

"I see a concrete cistern thing in the backyard, filled with dirt and plants, and my mom's T-shaped clothesline poles," I said. After thinking for a bit, I continued. "I see the fence line to the right, lots of alder and maple trees, a tree stump with huckleberries, lots of ferns, and my A-frame treehouse. My dad built that treehouse shortly after we moved into our house that he also built by himself," I said. I paused as the memories flooded back.

"There was a house right behind ours up on the hill. By the stump was a dirt pile. I didn't mind playing alone. I had imaginary friends, real to me. Johnny was nice, little like me. He would play with trucks in the dirt with me. Then there was John, the adult. I'm not sure why he was there with Johnny. He didn't play with us…he had a dark complexion, dark hair, very serious, not necessarily very friendly," I said.

Yvonne asked me to describe Johnny.

"Johnny looked like me, like a normal kid. I don't think they're related. I call John, Big Bad John, when that song came on, I thought of him," I said. Yvonne asked me to dig deeper and describe more.

"The woods to the right of our house probably go on for a mile. We would play there. Fun times and not fun times there," I said.

"What were the not fun times," asked Yvonne.

"The bad boys and girls built a fort on the hill to the right," I said.

"Were they neighbor kids?" asked Yvonne.

"They lived on the hill above us; we didn't know them. One time we went way out into the woods on a hike, and they held us prisoner for a while, and they hurt me (see "The Bad Boys and Girls" story in *Timeless Deja Vu*). They brought us to a dark gulley filled with junk, boards with nails. We got away. Then a wolf chased us up a big fir tree," I said. Most of the time we had fun. We would play army, pick huckleberries, and work on our tree fort.

"How long have you known Big John," asked Yvonne.

"Ever since I was little. I couldn't play with Johnny unless Big Bad John was there too. There was something magical about those woods. In the daytime. At night, very scary," I said.

"What made you afraid of the woods," asked Yvonne.

"I was afraid of the dark, had to have a light on, ended up often in my mom and dad's bed. They worked hard, and that made them tired, so they didn't wake up. My pretend playmates wanted me to come out and play at night. I would close the curtains tight so no one could see in my room. My cat kept me safe. Teddy and my other stuffed animals were standing watch. My cat slept on the pillow. My nightlight was a rocket ship (not surprisingly because of my love of outer space) that I won at a Sons of Norway bazaar. Sometimes I would wake up and couldn't breathe," I said. My mom always told me that sitting on the ground for too long in the backyard would bring on my croup. Several times a year, I would wake up and have difficulty breathing. I would cough, and it would sound like a baby seal. My mom would fill the bathtub with hot water, and I would breathe in the steam with a towel over my head. It was always frightening.

"You are safe now so that you can describe your emotions," said Yvonne.

"I would try to go back to sleep, but the pounding in my head was so loud that I couldn't sleep like my heartbeat was pounding through my pillow. I didn't want to open my eyes, hoped to make it through the night," I said. I liked to keep my sliding wooden closet doors open; there was something about it being closed that I didn't like.

"I have to keep the curtains closed. I was afraid of the darkness, and the dark things that come out at night," I said. Johnny wasn't afraid of the dark things in the backyard. I think that I always wanted the daylight to come soon, so I didn't have to be afraid.

"Why do you feel that you were afraid at night?" asked Yvonne.

"Things change at night. In the day I feel safe outside, and at night, I don't. Sometimes there is light out there, even though I'm afraid, I want to see that light. I don't know if I'm supposed to say," I said. I paused for a while.

"You're safe now. You can describe the light," said Yvonne.

"Something to do with Big Bad John. Not sure he wants me to say. Other little kids…they're afraid too. Some are already outside in the woods in the backyard by the light. I think they're from the neighborhood, not sure. I don't go to school with them. They wanted to see the light, that is why they are back there. I feel like I'm not supposed to say because maybe I won't be able to breathe," I said. Yvonne assured me that I was safe now.

"I told my little neighborhood friends that we should stay overnight in the A-frame tree fort behind my house, but they never did because they were afraid. I always thought of that fort as a spaceship," I said.

"Where is the light coming from?" asked Yvonne.

"On the hill above the stump, might be coming from my A-frame tree fort," I said.

"Any sounds or noise?" asked Yvonne.

15

"I'm listening, but no. Just regular night sounds," I said. It was then that I knew I was blocked from remembering any more information.

I had another hypnotherapy session with Yvonne on August 3, 2019, and we were able to push through the block we had experienced in June. She asked me to describe what I saw as I went back to 1964 at my house in Seattle.

"I'm outside of the house, steep driveway to the right, walking up the driveway. The front of our house has a sundeck. It's a brown house with cream-colored trim, and a tar and pea gravel roof." I go on to describe a sunny day, and the trees and garden, then I see the neighbor's house above ours on the hill. "I don't like that house. I liked to go and play with my trucks in the backyard, but I don't like that house up there. The people aren't nice, they pretend to be nice, and even fooled my parents because they're Norwegian too. I don't feel as safe as I used to because I know what goes on up there," I said. I talked about how the man who lived in that house would be alone with kids, including me, when his wife was gone. He wanted to play weird games and tried to give us Dixie cups filled with stuff that didn't smell right. Then he would hide in the closet and have us find him.

"He would say, 'Don't tell anybody about our little game, because whatever you're afraid of, that will come true.' He then asked us what we were most afraid of, and I said the devil because of what I had learned in Sunday school, and I was also afraid of not being able to breathe," I said.

"The devil will come and get you at night and make you stop breathing if you talk to anybody," he said.

I now know that I couldn't tell my parents because of that threat. I needed help. It wasn't just me that needed help because there were other kids in and out of that terrible house too.

"I remember the thing that saved me is the thing that I thought was scary, but it wasn't. I see a face, big head, upside-down tear shaped head, long slanted eyes, it's helping me and other kids," I said.

"Do you know the other kids?" asked Yvonne.

"No, they live up on the hill…I don't know them. The thing with a big head and slanted eyes, it wants to help and wants to know what is going on, but I was afraid," I said. I remembered the threat from the man on the hill. This thing spoke to me without using his mouth.

"I'm not the devil; it would be more accurate to say that he is the devil. Even though I might look scary to you, he is the bad one, not me," the entity said. I paused to think about what he said.

"What kind of clothes is he wearing?" asked Yvonne.

"It looks like a boxer's robe, shiny, fancy robes, it reminds me of that. He seems nice but strange and frightening looking, but so kind at the same time. He doesn't open his mouth; he talks directly to my mind," I said. I now know that this was an alien being, and he was using telepathy, of course.

"As you people say, you can't always judge a book by its cover," the alien said. Very true.

"The other kids are apprehensive, like me, most say they believe the slanted-eyed man, some don't," I said. I remember that in the daytime, saucer-shaped spacecraft in the blue sky by the clouds…they would come out when I was in the backyard to check in on me. I knew I was saved and knew that I didn't have to go to that house on the hill anymore. Before I could ask the question, the alien answered.

"You can tell your parents about me, but they may not understand. I am here for you and the other children. Your parents may not be prepared to hear about it. It is okay to tell your parents about that bad man, you must, nothing will happen to you, I will protect you," the alien said. I told my parents that I didn't want to go to the house on the hill anymore because they were mean. My mom understood, and I didn't have to say anything else. I felt protected after that, and I didn't have to worry about the bad man in that house.

"The alien showed us his technology in his spacecraft. I was already interested in space stuff. He showed me in my mind, like I'm just in the backyard, watching a TV screen in the air," I said. I think it was probably something like a hologram.

"I see the spaceship controls, and I told him that I wanted to fly, and he said that I would someday. It was golden inside, the lighting or maybe the mood, warm and safe," I said.

"Can you see dials or how to fly the thing?" asked Yvonne.

"There are windows, triangular windows, very minimal controls, less than fighter jets on Earth, or the inside of a space capsule, more open, nice design, not a lot of instruments like we use, more subdued like they don't have to touch the controls," I said.

"Any furniture in the spacecraft?" asked Yvonne.

"There were things to sit on, but more built into the structure itself, not like fighter pilot seats or furniture," I said.

I thought more deeply about this alien. He is a higher being, very benevolent, and loving. He told me that another would be assigned to me.

"Now you know what's possible, and you can help others. Be aware that when you tell people about this, they may not believe you," said the alien. The feeling I got was warm and I felt safe. The alien was showing me things, helping me, and teaching me. I did my best to understand, but it was a bit overwhelming. The other kids were looking at the same thing, like projections within a projection.

"Did he look familiar?" asked Yvonne.

"Yes. I encountered him earlier when I was younger…he has been checking in on me since my birth. In 1964, I was in danger, so he came to help. I always wanted to fly, so I did end up as a pilot in the military, but I didn't want to hurt people," I said. I paused as I choked up.

"Are you ready to stop for now?" asked Yvonne.

"I think so," I said. In my first session, I was blocked, not by the alien, but by the bad man on the hill. I estimate that there were 20 to 30 kids with the alien and me. Some kids didn't go with the alien because they were afraid of him. I don't know what happened to any of them. There was plenty to think about and discuss as I tried to put all this together.

Immediately after our hypnotic regression sessions, Yvonne usually conducts a debriefing. Each session with Yvonne gets more intense, and they build on previous sessions as I go deeper within myself. I reached a block in the June session and broke through in the August session. The neighbors who lived just above our house were friends with my parents. They were Norwegian, and I'll call them the Ronson family. The father was Roger, and the mother was Rigmor. They had three kids, two girls, and a boy around my age. Rigmor's parents were also friends with my parents, and they had been some of the original people in the neighborhood. A few years ago, my brother told me

19

that he met Rigmor's sister at a Sons of Norway function. He asked about Rigmor and Roger. Rigmor's sister told my brother that they don't speak to either of them anymore because Roger turned out to be a child molester. My brother was shocked, and I was speechless. I began to wonder if Roger was Big Bad John. It would seem to make sense based on my fear of the backyard and woods. I told Yvonne that I think Roger molested his kids and others, but I don't remember him molesting me.

I remember playing in the Ronson basement with the three kids, but then I suddenly stopped going up there and didn't want to play at their house anymore. I remember I ran away from their house when they were supposed to be babysitting me. I remember Mr. Ronson being alone with us kids in the basement. Roger was trying to be like a kid, but he wasn't, so that made me suspicious of him. There was also something wrong with the Ronson kids. They were weird and did strange things. He would try to give us weird juice that smelled funny. His kids and other kids drank it, but I refused. I think it was alcohol. I still have an aversion to drinking alcohol, and I don't take drinks from strangers. One of the creepiest things Mr. Ronson would do was to hide in closets in the basement, in the dark, and we were supposed to visit him in the dark closet and close the door. Kind of like hide and seek. I wouldn't do it and was afraid. The memory of this still gives me chills today. That is probably why I always kept my closet door open. I don't remember Rigmor being there; I think she was always gone from the house, probably running her small business. When I ran away from their house, it made my mom and dad upset because they didn't know what was going on and I didn't tell them very much other than I was afraid of being in the Ronson house. Eventually, my mom and dad figured out that something was wrong, and I didn't have to play with the Ronson kids or have their parents babysit me. Luckily, I don't think I was ever alone with Mr. Ronson. Those memories were frightening and contributed to the block I encountered in my first hypnotic regression session. I knew there was more to be uncovered and that the full story involved aliens.

As I was thinking about those retrieved and rekindled memories, I remembered the experience I had at the Contact in the Desert conference on Sunday, June 2, 2019. I woke up with a vision of a crystal blue-eyed, dark-complexioned, alien being in a dark robe. Behind and above him was a gigantic triangular spaceship. I spoke to my cosmic advisor Anzar on a spirit walk not long after I returned from the desert.

"Anzar, any more info on the crystal blue-eyed entity with triangle ship?" I asked.

"A hybrid, he just wanted to say hello," he said.

"And can I talk to him? He is neutral, right?" I asked.

"Yes."

"So, he won't harm my friends or me?"

"Correct."

"His name?"

"Ergot. E-R-G-O-T, pronounced Err-go," said Anzar.

"Hello, Ergot," I said. A few moments passed.

"Hello," said Ergot.

"Thank you for visiting me. Is there anything I can do to help?" I asked.

"No, just observing."

"Ok. I see you. So, is there anything you can tell me?" I asked.

"You have been taken before, in a reunion," he said.

"How young was I?"

"Anzar has not told you?"

"Kinda, wanted to hear it from you…wait, are you Big Bad John?" I asked in astonishment at my possible revelation. Ergo smiled, slightly amused. I turned to Anzar for an answer.

"Anzar? Is he?" I asked.

"Yes."

"So, he is neutral, yes?"

"Yes."

"You've been around for a long time?" I asked Ergot.

"Ha, yes," Ergot said.

"And you're a hybrid?"

"Yes."

"Why contact me?"

"In the neighborhood, and I thought I should show myself, so you have a better idea of what is going on," he said.

"When did I first get contacted?"

"As a baby." I was blown away by all this information.

On June 9, 2019, I took a spirit walk and asked my spirit friends about what happened in 1964.

"Did Mr. Ronson hurt me?" I asked.

"No," came the answer from my spirit guides. I didn't think so either, but I wanted to confirm with them.

"Weird things were going on in that basement. Anything more you can add to it? Did one of you intervene?" I asked.

"Yes," said Anzar.

"So, what I uncovered in hypnotherapy did happen?"

"Yes."

"Is Roger still alive?"

"No."

"Is Rigmor?"

"Yes," I told myself that I'd try to find them. I continued my conversation with my spirit guides.

"Big Bad John...that was you, Ergot?" I asked.

"Yes," said Ergot.

"Was it you with the golden spaceship? A golden triangle?"

"Yes."

"You showed me the controls?"

"No, that was not me." As it turned out, as confirmed by Anzar, the alien I first encountered in 1964 was Anzar. Ergot was assigned by Anzar to watch over me.

"No wonder I'm so interested in flying and outer space," I said.

"Yes."

"Did you protect me against the Ronsons?"

"Yes...your mom and dad suspected...we set up a force field," Ergot said.

"Tell me more about the golden triangle spaceship by the A-frame playhouse," I asked. But when I thought about it more, this made sense. An A-frame is a triangle. I wasn't abducted, I was saved. Anzar and Ergot were helping me.

"What do you think, Anzar?" I asked.

"Yes. Not abduction, because you wanted to go," he said.

"So, you're not completely neutral, you're neutral good, right Ergot?" I said. Ergot and Anzar smiled. I wanted to get my old friend Gene's opinion (he passed away in 2016).

"What do you think, Gene?" I asked.

"The Ronsons were terrible people that even hurt their own kids. Greed, money, worried about their view and value of their home," said Gene.

"Did they ever molest me?" I asked.

"No, but others, yes. I'm sorry that happened to you," said Gene. I tried to locate the Ronson's, but none of them are on Google, FaceBook, White Pages, Find a Grave, or on any online search. It's almost as though they all just disappeared.

On August 4th, I spoke to Anzar and my spirit friends again.

"Anzar, were you the tall alien with the narrow-slanted eyes?" I asked. I didn't get an answer. I decided to ask my friend, Gene, directly.

"Was it Anzar?" I asked.

"Why wouldn't it be?" said Gene. I laughed. So, it was Anzar. The being who stepped in to rescue me was Anzar, in one of his many forms.

"Thank you, Gene. Thank you, Anzar, really, thank you," I said.

Anzar smiled.

"To confirm, the image I had of the tall alien with narrow slanted eyes in 1964 was you, Anzar?"

"Yes," said Anzar.

"And Ergot was who you assigned?"

"Yes."

"It was you who showed me the ship, right, Anzar?"

"Yes."

I was satisfied. The second regression session was a success, and we now had a more complete story.

The bottom line to this story is that once again, I was rescued by an alien–Anzar in a different form along with an alien hybrid named Ergot. They were initially attracted to our neighborhood because of the Nike site. It all made sense. The enormity of this hit me: Ergot is Big Bad John, and it was Ergot who was assigned to protect me and helped me stay away from Roger. The spaceship had other kids in it, perhaps the others who were saved. Then I thought of the song "Big Bad John." In that song, Big Bad John holds up the timbers in the collapsing mine so all the other miners can get out. In other words, despite his frightening reputation as a tough guy, Big Bad John saved people, so he wasn't so bad after all. You really can't always judge a book by its cover. Jimmy Dean recorded the hit song in 1961. Here is the last verse:

"Now, they never reopened that worthless pit
They just placed a marble stand in front of it

These few words are written on that stand
At the bottom of this mine lies a big, big man
Big John
(Big John, Big John)
Big Bad John (Big John)
(Big John) Big Bad John"

My Menagerie (1966)

I've worked in both military and maximum-security civilian prisons. I know what it's like to be locked up, at least for a shift. And although I don't know what it's like to be confined to a wheelchair, I do know what it's like to be trapped by one's own fears. "The Menagerie," a two-part episode of the original *Star Trek* TV series, has always freaked me out. I was literally afraid to watch it when I was younger and have largely avoided watching it since. Just recently, I watched it in its entirety and thought about what was causing me to avoid this well-made, award-winning episode. Initially, I thought the reason might have been because of how hideously scarred and injured Captain Pike was and how sad the story was, but I doubt that was the reason because I had seen much worse in other shows and movies. I needed to get to the bottom of this perplexing conundrum.

"The Menagerie" was first broadcast in November 1966. The show was built around the original *Star Trek* pilot "The Cage" that was rejected by the network. Executive producer and creator Gene Roddenberry wanted to salvage the original pilot, so he wrote a wraparound or envelope story. The two-part episode (the only two-parter in the series) tells the story of Spock risking his career to kidnap his former captain, Christopher Pike, and return him to the forbidden planet of Talos IV. Pike had been severely injured and maimed in a training exercise and was confined to a wheelchair. Spock commandeers the Enterprise along with the crew, Captain Kirk, and Commodore Mendez. A court-martial is convened as Spock has locked the controls, which won't allow Captain Kirk to regain control of the ship.

Spock then presents his evidence in the form of a video signal from Talos IV. The tribunal watches as Captain Pike's story is presented to them. In the video, they see Pike and his landing party beamed down to Talos IV to help a group of survivors. It turns out that the Talosians created the illusion of the survivors to lure Captain Pike to the surface of the planet. Pike is captured by the aliens and taken below the surface. He is put in a cage with a beautiful young woman named Vina, the only human survivor left. The remaining crew of the Enterprise attempt to rescue Captain Pike while the Talosians do everything they can to convince him to stay by offering Vina as his mate and punishing him for wrong thinking. When he resists his captors, the aliens capture two female Enterprise crewmembers to entice Pike. Eventually, Captain Pike captures one of the Talosians and takes him and the others to the surface. It's then that the Talosians realize that humans aren't reliable and manageable for their purposes to repopulate the planet. Pike and the Enterprise crew leave, but Vina must stay behind because she is kept beautiful and alive by the Talosians. Once this story has been presented to Captain Kirk, Commodore Mendez, and Captain Pike, it becomes clear that the Talosians want to bring Pike back to stay with Vina. The gruesomely injured Pike agrees and then Commodore Mendez disappears since he was only an illusion to begin with.

When I watched this episode recently, all these years later, I can see what was truly disturbing me. My apprehension about watching this episode was deep-seated within me. I've probably watched every other original *Star Trek* episode 50 times, but I avoided "the Menagerie" consistently. It was the aliens. The powerful illusions and control of the minds of humans are what scared me the most. I also was fearful of their appearance: large bulbous heads and skinny feminine bodies. I now know that these Talosians reminded me of the aliens I had met. I was completely helpless, like Captain Pike, in their hands. I wasn't ready to deal with my alien contact until now. The underlying subconscious fear that lay beneath my seemingly irrational fear of "the Menagerie" has now come to the surface of my consciousness and could be considered further evidence of my being abducted by actual aliens. Or, perhaps, could all this be an illusion?

Special Processing (1973)

Why me? That is the question that many experiencers, meaning those people who have been abducted or contacted by alien beings, ask. It's a fair question. I've contemplated the answer to this question. Was I chosen at random—maybe just in the wrong place at the wrong time? Is there something special about me? Am I cursed? Is it my blood type? Is it a family tradition or genetic in some way? The answer may be all the above. There were at least four paranormal experiences that my gut told me needed to be explored further under hypnotic regression. Those incidents (some written about in my first two *Timeless* books) took place in 1964, 1973, 1977, and 1978. For this story, I revisited my experience detailed in "My Nazi Aunt" found in *Timeless Deja Vu*. In that story from 1973, I remembered Aunt Walborg (my dad's youngest sister), whom I call my Nazi aunt, visiting me in my bedroom at Christmas time ostensibly for sexual purposes. I also remember that there were small beings, presumably of alien origin, with her. But, my dear readers, there is more to the story.

On May 4, 2019, I had a hypnotherapy session with Yvonne Smith. We delved into the incident with my Nazi aunt, and, as both Yvonne and I suspected, some significant details were missing from my original account. My hypnotic regression took me back to Christmas time 1973.

"I'm in my childhood home in Seattle, in the living room opening presents. My mom and dad are there, and so are my little nephews. My sister and her husband, along with my aunt Walborg and Uncle Ragnar, are drinking too much."

Mom didn't mind people having a drink but didn't like them to be drunk. She lost her father, who was an alcoholic, to suicide.

"Walborg is playing with my nephews (my sister's kids) on the floor and spraying them with her French perfume. It's such a strong smell that it's choking me. Aunt Walborg is an attractive woman for her age, and her dress is very short and very tight. I can tell that my mom disapproves," I said.

"After opening presents, my sister, my brother-in-law, and her kids are preparing to leave. My mom is worried because my sister and her husband had been drinking, and she didn't want them to drive, especially with their kids in the car. They drive away despite my mom's urgent suggestion that they spend the night." At around 10 pm, I gathered my presents and said goodnight to everyone and headed for my bedroom downstairs. It was a typical, traditional Norwegian Christmas eve—lutefisk dinner, wash up, then open presents. In those days, people smoked in the house, so I remember the house smelled like smoke. That was another thing my mom disapproved of because she always told me: "Don't smoke and don't drink." I plopped my presents on my table and put on my pajamas. My bed was just to the right of the bedroom door facing a large window. Tiger, my big tabby cat, followed me and took near-complete ownership of my pillow as I laid my head down. I heard voices upstairs as I fell asleep.

"I was startled awake because Tiger jumped off my bed. He was a heavy cat, and it was very noticeable when he jumped on or off the bed. I looked to my left, and there was my aunt in the doorway, backlit with the faint lighting coming from the stairway behind her and to the right. I don't seem to be able to move," I said.

Yvonne asked me to look in the doorway and describe what I see.

"My aunt is wearing a white dress, the same one she had been wearing, tight-fitting, and short. She isn't wearing shoes, and she is just staring at me, but I can't move or even say anything," I said.

Yvonne asked me to describe my aunt's face.

"It's in the darkness, I stare at her, but it doesn't look like her. What I see is the shape of her, but the face looks wrong like it's put together incorrectly. The eyes, face, and mouth are off, like an abstract painting. Her face is contorting, morphing, scrambled. It's frightening," I said.

Yvonne asked me to describe her hair.

"More like a helmet, because it's so flat. Now I'm looking at the thing but can't move," I said.

Yvonne asked what position I was in.

"Now, I'm upright, but not doing it myself, and I'm facing the doorway. It's almost like the helmet has a mask on it. Like a fighter pilot, a dark shield, oxygen mask, but more complicated looking, not normal. It's hiding the distorted face. No longer my aunt, something else," I said. I realized that this was not my aunt anymore. Maybe she was there initially, but not now. "The thing is wearing something like a uniform. I'm standing there and can't move," I said.

Yvonne prompts me to describe my surroundings.

"Weird lighting, not dark, not light, bluish light, coming from behind the being, the thing, whatever it is. My cat is gone, I want him there, he protects me. I'm being stood up by a force," I said.

Yvonne asked if there were others in the room.

"Yes. There are others in the room, like stick figures, very thin—maybe, six of them, maybe more. They are following the person with a mask, the one causing this to happen," I said. I thought more deeply about the entity in my room, and it brought fear and dread to mind.

"A tail, that thing has a tail, the one with the mask, yeah, big thick tail, like a lizard. Not good, not a good thing, not at all, it doesn't care anything about me, my cat, or my family. My aunt brought it here. Brought them here," I said.

Yvonne reminded me that I'm safe now, and to describe what I see.

"These smaller things around me, they're not in charge, they're supporting me, but not touching me. I'm now lying down, but they aren't touching me, but holding me up," I said.

Yvonne asked if I was in my bedroom.

"No. Not familiar, not my bedroom, darker place, super-moist environment, very warm, swamp-like," I said.

Yvonne asked what I see around me.

"Confined space, lying down position, can't move, rotating around inside of a confined space. Very moist like a sauna, greenish colors, dark. Not much light, inside of a disc, pylon in the middle, rotating around, 3D disc, sloped top and bottom, triangular panels in the top part of the disk, sense of movement, moving fast, looks like the night sky, definitely not in my room," I said.

Yvonne asked if I can provide more detail.

"Inside of this disc, the pylon is central to this whole thing, not sure why. I'm anesthetized, I can't react, my mind is slowing down, fuzzy thinking, still lying down, but I can't feel anything on my back," I said.

Yvonne asked me to use my body memory and remember if there was any pressure on my body.

"My body memory is telling me that it's my abdomen. I've always been sensitive there. Don't want to remember, because it hurt," I said.

Yvonne assured me that I wouldn't feel the pain now as I remembered and that I was safe. She wanted me to pinpoint the cause of the pressure.

"Pressure on my abdomen. Something is pushing or poking around," I said.

Yvonne asked what it was.

"Looks like a lawn dart, those things that are now illegal. Poking and pushing inside of me, but not being held, levitated, no one touching it," I said.

Yvonne said I could relax and go deeper and describe the beings around me.

"The thing with a tail is gone, I call him the transportation chief. His job was done, but now another being enters the picture," I said. I paused to take in the images.

"The mask isn't a mask. The face is so hideous; it's a praying mantis, a bug, one of the things around me. I'm floating above myself, trying to look at this scene from above. A grasshopper/praying mantis, expressionless face, warm environment, dim lights," I said. I paused for a few moments and wondered what my aunt has to do with this.

"The other things or beings don't seem significant, like worker ants, the bug is in charge. I'm so anesthetized, I want to scream out, but I can't. I'm being told 'You don't need to know,' by the bug. I had a lot of questions, but he answered before I could ask," I said. I paused as I remembered the scene and experienced the emotions again.

Yvonne asked me if there were any other sensations or pressure.

"I have a headache," I said.

Yvonne told me to allow myself to remember without pain or discomfort.

"There is like a clamp or device holding my head. It's too tight, not sure what it's doing, very uncomfortable. Dull pain still going on in my abdomen," I said. Yvonne asked if there was any movement near my head.

"Yes, little things, the bug is directing everything, sometimes touching me, sometimes making things touch me, greenish light the whole time. They don't seem to be that concerned about me or saying very much. It's telepathy only," I said.

Yvonne asked me what I sensed they were thinking?

"The bug says that I'm special. He is telling the others to be careful, because they were clumsy and hurt me," I said.

Yvonne asked if the bug seems familiar.

"Yeah, I think I've seen him before," I said. "I find bugs that look like him, Jerusalem crickets, and I find them when I'm digging, not a human face, but oddly recognizable to me, it shocks me how familiar he is. The small entities are clumsy. The head brace was removed. The bug ordered them to remove it," I added.

"The bug is a doctor. He was upset with them. Special processing is what I'm being told. Whatever that means. That's what the doctor says," I said. Then I thought about this more deeply and began connecting the dots. Is this why I'm so afraid of medical procedures? My conscious mind intruded again, what does it have to do with my aunt? I think it was because she called them.

"No pressure on the abdomen, no, they're done with special processing, things spinning around the pylon thing, a lot of movement. I wake up, sore, head hurts," I said.

Yvonne asked me how long this lasted and if I can see a clock in my room.

"Yes, it's an old flip number clock. Yes, 12:54. Cat is back, on my pillow, big fat cat, nice to know he's there," I said.

Yvonne asked me if there was anything else I needed to verbalize at this time.

"No, just confused, how I remember things," I said.

As I awoke from the hypnosis, I was surprised how much I remembered from the session. It was all very clear, everything I was saying and thinking. But how does my aunt fit in? I saw my aunt, but, as Yvonne said, perhaps that was a screen memory, and maybe not her at all. Aliens will put a picture in your mind to mask their activities. The critical bit of evidence is that my cat jumped off the bed. Yvonne reminded me that animals detect dangerous events before they happen.

Yvonne asked if there had been any other instances of my aunt showing up in my room. As far as I could remember, this was the only time. I just pieced things together because she gave me money for a car a year later when I was 16, which made my parents upset. I thought it was a bribe to stay quiet. She did seem to stare at me, but maybe that is transference since I was noticing how attractive and alluring my aunt was in 1973. The money she gave me for my car, and later in 1991 when I stayed with her in Oslo after Uncle Ragnar died, she was buying me clothes and taking me to fancy dinners, and having me use her private bath, all of that seemed to fit into my idea that she was interested in me sexually. I realize that this is all circumstantial evidence, but I had drawn some type of conclusion from this. I can admit that the sexual overtones might have been coming from me and not her. I also thought that maybe it was like during the German occupation of Norway when the Nazis gave her everything to gain her allegiance and become a Gestapo agent. In that regard, she wanted me close to her and to be on her side. She even wanted me to name my first-born child after her. She wanted an heir and a legacy.

After thinking about this for the two nights after the hypnotic regression, I've concluded that Aunt Walborg was in my doorway briefly on Christmas Eve in 1973, and she may have touched me, but I don't think there was sex involved. The real significance of the event was that it was alien abduction masked by a screen memory. She may have opened an inter-dimensional doorway, perhaps even unknowingly. My cousin Kanum told me that Aunt Walborg had psychic experiences in her life, especially at our house up north.

In one of my visions the night after the regression therapy, the bug doctor came into my thoughts.

"So, you think you know what is going on?" asked the doctor in a mocking tone. That was rather ominous. Also, in the evening after the regression, when I was having dinner with my cousin Brita in San Diego (who is also an experiencer by the way), I was talking about the bug doctor when I noticed something happening behind Brita. We were sitting outside, and on a column, there was a conduit leading to an electrical outlet. It was swinging wildly back and forth. No one had brushed by it or touched it; the conduit swung on its own. I mentioned it to Brita, but it stopped shortly after that. I got up and examined the conduit to make sure it wasn't the wind that was causing it to move. No wind and nobody walked by. It wasn't easy to move back and forth either as I tested the conduit. Freaky. I'm not sure what the bug doctor meant by special processing, but I guess I'll find out. I do know this; I've been terrified of doctor and dentist visits for as long as I could remember. Seriously scared. I must put on my big boy pants every time I go to an appointment. My blood pressure always spikes when I enter a medical facility. I think I now know the reason why.

La Grange Park (1974)

Hey, daddy-o
I don't want to go down to the basement
There's somethin' down there
I don't want to go/Hey, Romeo
There's somethin' down there
I don't want to go down to the basement.

– The Ramones, "I Don't Want to Go Down to the Basement"

My sister Bjørg and her family moved to La Grange Park, Illinois, a Chicago suburb, in 1974. I flew out to spend four weeks with them that summer. I'm sure it was nice for my parents to get some time away from me. La Grange Park was farmland until 1860 when the five original farmers started building a few homes. Many more families came to the area after the Chicago Fire in 1871 (thanks to Mrs. O'Leary's cow), so the farmers sold more land to build houses. Alphonse H. Kemman and Pete Swanson are credited with further developing La Grange Park when they decided to sell alcohol to supplement their income. Their drinking establishment was called a blind pig, later in the 1920s to be called a speakeasy. The neighbors vehemently complained about the noise and raucous behavior of the bar patrons. In 1892, La Grange Park was incorporated. One of the first regulations was to ban the sale of alcohol. The community grew dramatically after 1943, with its present population being 13,300. Allan B. Calhamer, a former mail carrier and the man who invented the board game Diplomacy, grew up in La Grange Park.

Mobster Anthony J. Battaglia was gunned down in his driveway not far from my sister's house. He was the brother of Chicago crime boss Sam "Teets" Battaglia. Neighbors who heard the shots failed to identify the assassin. Anthony had been retired for 13 years before he was killed. His family was asked by reporters what business Anthony had retired from, but they, not surprisingly, declined to comment.

Bjørg lived in a red brick, three-story duplex, probably built in the 1940s. It had a garage and a huge backyard with tall trees all around. It was a nice place. There was another duplex to the south, and there was a sidewalk and a chain-link fence and gate separating the homes on each side. Each of these duplex units had a daylight basement with windows high up on the walls that let in light.

On the third story, my sister and her husband Carl had their master bedroom, and my two little nephews shared a small bedroom. There was also a bathroom. A steep carpeted staircase descended to the middle floor with a large kitchen, living room, and dining room. Then there was a door to the basement with old wooden steps. I slept in a spare bed in the basement along with the washer and dryer, the furnace, water heater, and a play area for the boys. I noticed right away that it was creepy in that basement. I heard lots of strange noises at night—the pipes, the water heater, the air conditioning ducts, the settling of the house, and sometimes what sounded like people outside. I would wake up frightened every night and even came upstairs and slept on the sofa a few times.

One night there was a terrible lightning storm. The thunderclaps woke me up, and I could hear that the dangerous storm was coming closer and closer. CRACK! BOOM! It sounded like lightning hit the house as the whole structure shook, and the windows in the basement rattled. I ran upstairs to my sister's room. She was laughing at me, and so was her husband Carl. We figured out that the lightning bolt had hit the big oak tree in the backyard. There were several more lightning strikes until the storm moved on, and I reluctantly headed back down to the basement.

It wasn't all frightful. I had some fun times staying with my sister that summer. We went to baseball games at Wrigley Field to see the Chicago Cubs and to old Comiskey Park to see the Chicago White Sox. I saw Billy Williams play for the Cubs and Dick Allen play for the White Sox—two of my favorites. I remember Carl not wanting to pay for stadium parking at Comiskey, so we parked in the projects in the southside of Chicago and walked quite a distance. Scary neighborhood. I got to take the train in and out of the city. My sister took me to the Sears Tower, the tallest building in the United States at the time, and we went for dinner at a fancy French restaurant in the Chicago Loop downtown. I ordered Beef Wellington and *pâté de foie gras*. Delicious.

Other things held my interest, as well. I was beginning to be intensely aware of girls that summer. Maybe obsessed is a better word. My nephews' babysitter was an incredibly beautiful girl of 18, but I never even spoke to her. I just wasn't very good at that sort of thing. The next-door neighbor kids, Marco and Paul, were nice, and I buddied up with them for a while when I was there. They were a few years older and more experienced than I was. Their stories of date conquests intrigued me, and Marco and Paul seemed to know all the secrets about those beautiful and mysterious creatures. But I could only dream because I believed there was no way a girl would be interested in me.

I kept hearing the strange noises every night, and increasingly the outside noises worried me even more. In the middle of the night, I would hear footsteps sliding along the sidewalk on the side of the house and the rusty chain-link gate opening and closing. Who would be walking out there between the houses in the middle of the night? I told my young friends next door about this, and they told me the neighbors on the other side of us had a mentally ill son in his 20s.

"He lives in the basement, they keep him locked up there because he's criminally insane and has killed people," said Marco. I paused to take this in.

"Wait, wouldn't he be in prison?" I asked.

"They couldn't prove it, and his mom hides him away," said Paul.

"Have you heard him walking around or seen him?" I asked.

"Yeah, one time, scared the shit outta me, so I don't go near that side of the house anymore," said Marco.

"Oh, great, I sleep in the basement on that side of the house," I said.

"You're braver than me," said Paul. I thought about this new revelation. Would I survive the summer with mafia hits in our neighborhood and a criminally insane murderer roaming the streets at night?

"The footsteps I hear sound like an old man, sliding along, slowly," I said.

"Yeah, he's got a club foot, and drags it," said Marco.

A few days later, I woke up in the middle of the night again. I heard the hissing of the water heater, the air conditioning ducts were rattling, and gusts of wind outside causing the tree branches to scratch against the side of the house and the roof. The settling of the house left me unsettled. Then, outside, I heard the rusty gate latch being unfastened and swinging open. Was the wind blowing it open? No. I heard those sliding footsteps, methodical, slow, menacing. The gate suddenly slammed shut, rattling the basement window on that side. I peeked out from under my covers and saw a shadow moving slowly past the window facing the sidewalk. I could see what looked like pajama pants and slippers. I dared not go up to the window for a closer look. The sliding steps stopped in front of the second basement window. The wind gained strength and howled mercilessly. All the sounds of the house seemed to reach a crescendo of frightening proportions. The person outside the window knelt and tested my window to see if it would open. Thank God it was latched. I grabbed my baseball bat for protection as my heart was racing, and my breathing was rapid like a rabbit. The person straightened up again and continued back through the gate, closing it carefully. Oh God, I survived, thank you! I made a break for it and ran up the basement steps with my blanket. From that night on, I slept in the living room.

I told my sister the next day, and she said that the boys next door were using their imaginations a bit too much. Carl just laughed.

"They got you but good," he said, continuing to laugh. I laughed nervously, smiling. I told Marco and Paul what happened, and they said that I was lucky that the window latch was secured; otherwise, I would have been dead.

"So, it wasn't you guys trying to scare me? That's what Carl thinks," I said.

"No way, I'm not going out there at night. Are you crazy?" said Paul.

"Me neither, let 'em kill some other sucker," said Marco. Although this scary basement experience still chills me today when I think about it, the good fright served as a nice distraction that kept me from obsessing too much about another deep mystery—girls.

Mel's Hole (1977)

This story, and the other alien stories in this book, are different than the other stories I've written in my first two *Timeless* books. In this case, instead of relying solely on my memory, I contacted an old friend to see what he could remember from 42 years ago. I also asked for help from my spirit guides, and from a world-renowned hypnotherapist named Yvonne Smith. She specializes in alien abductions and encounters. I can tell you this, never in a million years did I think I would be telling stories of alien abductions or that I would undergo hypnosis. I've had a serious fear of being hypnotized for as long as I can remember. I mean, who wants to be made to act like a chicken and humiliated in front of a crowd? Not me. I changed my mind and was willing, in part, because this spiritual awakening I've been going through the past three years keeps presenting me with new information and new challenges, and because Yvonne comes highly recommended and is most trustworthy. Some of this story is from conscious memories, while other memories have been stimulated by discussions with my friend and remain a bit fuzzy, and the rest have been recovered through the skillful hypnotic regression therapy with Yvonne. My friend agrees with some of my telling of the story, disagrees with other parts, and isn't quite sure about the rest.

In the summer of 1977, my friend Ernie and I took a road trip. We planned to drive to Salt Lake City, Utah, then to the Grand Canyon, Las Vegas, Los Angeles, and finally make the long drive up the west coast and back home to Seattle. We drove in my parents' 1972 red Volvo station wagon. My friends called that car, "the Brick." On the morning we left, my old childhood friend Monte showed up. I hadn't seen him for more than seven years. He drove up in a muscle car, a late 1960s Camaro, I think

47

it was. By the way, Camaro means friend or pal in French. It seemed rather odd that he would appear randomly just as I was about to take off on the road trip. Monte didn't stay long, and it might have been because I wasn't friendly. I'm not sure why. Maybe it's because we change as we grow older, without realizing it, so our old friends whom we haven't had much contact with seem different and less familiar. It was then that I noticed big black birds flying overhead; at first, I thought they were crows, but now I believe they were ravens. After Monte left, I was ready and drove to Ernie's house to pick him up and start our trip.

Probably around 11 o'clock in the late morning, we had crossed over Snoqualmie Pass. I remember telling Ernie that my mother used to ski at Snoqualmie Summit ski area, but that it was too tame for me. The slopes were not challenging enough. At the top of the big chair at Snoqualmie ski area was the Thunderbird Lodge. We stopped at the summit to use the public restroom. Again, I noticed the big black birds. I thought it was weird, but we continued on Interstate 90 to Ellensburg and crossed over into eastern Washington. We then took the exit for Highway 82 to Yakima. I remember that we stopped shortly after that, probably to eat something. Our budget problem led me to live off cheese sandwiches with thousand island dressing, cereal, candy, Mother's cookies, nuts, apples, and Wyler's fruit juice mix. Poor diet and lack of sleep may have doomed our trip from the get-go. We drove off the highway on a dirt road and stopped. It was some type of vista viewpoint. Although I didn't know it then, I now know that the place we stopped was Manastash Ridge, the supposed location of the infamous, Mel's Hole.

In 1997, a man named Mel Waters was interviewed on the *Coast to Coast AM* radio show with Art Bell. He claimed that he owned some land on Manastash Ridge in Kittitas County, near Ellensburg, Washington. On his property, some bizarre things were going on attributed to a hole in the ground, then known as the Devil's Hole. Mel said that the hole measured nine feet in diameter with hand-laid bricks lining the rim down to about 15 feet. The hole then drops off to an unknown depth. Mr. Waters claimed that Native Americans, who felt the hole was cursed, and early settlers knew of the anomaly that had no bottom. Mel said that he never heard anything he threw down the hole to hit bottom. Animals refused to go near it. The mystery became known as Mel's Hole. Mel was on *Coast to Coast* several more times and finally said that a government official told him that he wasn't allowed near the hole. Eventually, Mr. Waters moved to Australia and leased the property to the government. Mel never gave away the exact location of his hole. In 2008, a Native American medicine man named Red Elk claimed that he had visited the hole as a boy and corroborated Mel's story. Red Elk went on to say that Mel's Hole was an underground UFO base and that he had witnessed a UFO hovering over the hole. Since no one has ever located Mel's Hole and Mel Waters is not even known to be a real person, it remains a mystery. I don't remember anything strange happening as we ate our sandwiches on Manastash Ridge, but I did notice some more large black birds. I was pretty sure that they were ravens because of the gravel-throated croaking sounds they made.

We continued our trip on highway 82 to Yakima and eventually merging on to highway 84 in Oregon as we headed into the Blue Mountains. Everything seemed to be going well until we neared an overpass just outside of Boise, Idaho. It was getting dark, Ernie was driving, and we were both sleepy. I woke up to a truck horn blaring, and when I opened my eyes, I saw a semi-truck bearing down on us. We were in the wrong lane and headed straight for him. I quickly looked over at Ernie, and he was asleep.

"Ernie!" I yelled as loud as I could, and then I'm not sure if I grabbed the wheel or he swerved at the last minute, but either way, we avoided a fatal head-on collision. Thinking about this incident even today is frightening—what a close call. I remember getting angry at Ernie, but that was unfair of me because we were both tired and neither one of us should have been driving.

Somewhere around Black Pine Peak, Idaho, we decided to camp for the night. We took one of the side roads from the highway that we thought led to a forest campground, but we never made it there. It was dark, and we either drove past the campground, or it was much further than we thought it was. Near a clearing, we pulled over to the side of the dirt road. We were too tired to put up a tent, so we decided to sleep as best we could in the car. After some grape flavored Wyler's drink and an apple, I unzipped my sleeping bag and placed it over me in the driver's seat, and then I tilted the seat back as far as it would go. It was okay for about 20 minutes, and then it became almost intolerable. I was too tall, and the seat didn't recline enough, and the steering wheel bruised my ribs. Ernie and I fell into a restless and uncomfortable sleep.

There was nobody else around as we attempted to sleep in the pitch-black darkness on the side of that forest road. I kept waking up to strange noises. I identified some of the sounds to be owls, coyotes, and trees being blown in the wind that had picked up. Just when I thought I drifted off to sleep, another strange noise. As the night wore on, I began to have this overwhelming feeling of doom that I couldn't shake. It wasn't the usual caution and watchfulness that I had from backpacking in the wilderness and encountering wild animals, including bears; this was something unnatural and spookier. I kept sensing that someone or something was watching us from the tree line. A few times I woke up to what I thought were flashlights going on and off, but I didn't see anyone. Ernie thought that at one point there might

50

have been a car or truck driving up and shining its lights, but he wasn't sure. In my restless moments of sleep, I had weird dreams of people surrounding our car, but they weren't ordinary people, they were smaller, skinnier, and seemed non-human.

During my hypnotic regression, Yvonne asked me to think more about the sights, sounds, and smells. As I placed myself back in time under hypnosis, I noticed that it was windy, and there were more strange lights around us, but the ravens that had followed us were gone. I heard a whooshing sound, then some mechanical sounds, followed by the smell of rain, but it wasn't raining. Yvonne asked me to look to my right in the passenger seat and tell her what I saw. I was shocked, and a bit frightened, as I remembered.

"Ernie is gone! Where is he?" I said. His disappearance freaked me out after I said it because I hadn't consciously remembered that before.

"The day was all night," I told Yvonne. That night seemed to go on forever. I was frozen and paralyzed and couldn't get up to look for Ernie, although I wanted to.

"What else do you see," Yvonne asked.

"Tall beings, dark, in robes, but I can't see their faces— lights shining down from the sky, powerful lights. I'm afraid, but I can't move," I said.

That night, after my hypnotherapy, I had a powerful dream vision. I was able to get out of the car, but it was unclear how. Did I float out? The next thing I knew, I was walking on the dirt road and saw a small being with a hat and a long coat. He looked like the little being I saw in a vision I had on Halloween 2018, standing on the road below our house looking up at us. It was frightening. Back to the incident in 1977, I was giving the

51

small being a report. Ernie eventually returned to the car after what may have been hours (lost time) but was acting strangely and I couldn't make much sense of what he was saying. I then drifted off into a deep sleep.

Was I abducted? Was Ernie abducted? I asked my spirit guides Theodora and Ozzie, my spirit friends Gene and Maia, and my alien mystic advisor Anzar because they had told me previously that I've never been abducted, just contacted several times. They then clarified things for me.

"It wasn't an abduction; it was a reunion." What? I guess you must be very specific when asking questions, something my wife Ginger has tried to teach me.

"An abduction means you were taken unwillingly, but you were willing. You're a hybrid, so it is a reunion," they added. Wow, a hybrid. I've dealt with this revelation before in my story "Anzar's Answers" in *Timeless Deja Vu*.

"So, you didn't want me to have all this information right away because it would spin me off kilter?" I asked.

"Yes," was the answer.

"Well, I'm ready," I said. They paused for a moment.

"The black birds represent the aliens, they led you to that place," said my spirit guides. That seemed to make sense.

"What happened to Ernie?" I asked.

"He was abducted," they said.

"Was he experimented on…like on a spaceship?"

"Yes."

"Was I with them in the ship?"

52

"Yes,"

"I went with them willingly?"

"Yes."

"Gene?" I asked, hoping for even more clarification as my concern for not wanting to be the bad guy in this story increased.

"We are the aliens," said Gene. I smiled.

"I know, you told me, so that means me too," I said.

"Of course," he said. Then I thought for a moment.

"Wait, are you saying I facilitated this abduction of Ernie?" I asked. They paused again.

"Yes," they said.

"Please tell me that I didn't do it to be mean," I said as my fears of being the bad guy seemed to be confirmed.

"No, you did not," they said. I was putting it all together and feeling somewhat relieved.

"So, this is what happened when we were parked off the side of the road that night?" I asked.

"Yes."

"How long were we gone?"

"A while." I thought back to the near-death collision with the semi-truck near Boise, the close call that still haunts me to this day.

"Did you help us in Boise," I asked.

"Yes, we woke you up," they said. I thanked them all and was still reeling from the information I had confirmed and received.

"Is it so hard to believe one more miraculous thing when you already believe in other extraordinary things?" asked Gene. I smiled because Gene had a way of getting right to the point.

"You're right," I said as I laughed. When I thought more about the short being whom I reported to, I remembered that he wasn't very nice, just like in my vision on Halloween. I got a creepy and bad feeling from him.

"They don't necessarily like you talking and writing about this," added my spirit guides.

I don't mean any harm. I want to help people and tell them what is going on. I wanted more details of that night.

"Did an alien spaceship land in the clearing?" I asked.

"Yes," my spirit guides said.

"The lights, the whooshing sound?"

"Yes."

"I saw other beings, tall, in dark robes?" I asked to verify.

"Yes," they told me.

"I don't want to do bad things. I'm good, like my comic book character Snarc. I am Snarc, as Ginger once said." Just to clarify, Snarc was an alien hybrid comic book character I created in 1982. My comic strip was published in the Montana Tech *Technocrat* newspaper (I still have copies). In 2018, my second eldest son created a 3D Snarc for me as a Christmas present using his 3D printer. That inspired me to revive the character, and I published the new adventures of Snarc in 2019 with the help of illustrator Gary Dumm. The tagline is: "half-alien, half-human, all heart."

"Yes," all connected, they said.

"The master aliens were the big ones? And I don't see their faces."

"Yes."

"You guys said I was taken to the ship, but you didn't mention that the aliens did any experiments on me."

"No, you had already been processed." I thought for a moment.

"Wait, what does that mean?" I asked.

"They had already done that before," my spirit guides said.

"So, when was my original abduction processing or reunion?"

"1964 and 1973," came the answer (see "My Nazi Aunt" in *Timeless Deja Vu*). This exchange of information was a lot for me to take in. I needed a break.

There was more to the road trip than just the first day and night. In some ways, I think the trip seemed to be overshadowed and cursed by the strange events of the first night on the road. We argued a lot. I blame myself more than Ernie for that. We did, however, have fun in Salt Lake City with Ernie's Uncle Darwin. He had a Chuck Berry guitar and amplifier and played us a tune or two. Uncle Darwin took us rafting on the Green River in an old army surplus raft, and we set up camp by the river. The rapids were more turbulent and dangerous than we had imagined. After our Salt Lake City adventures, Ernie and I visited Bryce Canyon and the Grand Canyon.

We made a stop in Las Vegas, but we were too broke to get a hotel room, so we spent the afternoon in a public swimming pool to avoid the heat. I remember the sound of cicadas; it was almost deafening. We spotted comedienne Joan Rivers walking on the strip. Our next stop was Los Angeles. I think I was an asshole at this point. We were going to stay with Ernie's other uncle in his beach house, but something fell through, so we ended up sleeping in the car on Mt. Wilson instead. Not too smart given what had happened last time we slept in the car and the fact that the cops could bust us for vagrancy. We were able to go swimming at Will Rogers State Beach the next day, which was fun. I remember some little kid with a magnifying glass who was burning girls with their bikini top straps off lying on their stomachs. They jumped up, and you get the idea. One of the pleasant memories I had from the road trip was listening to our cassette mix tapes: Rush, Jethro Tull, Genesis, King Crimson, Emerson, Lake & Palmer, Rick Wakeman, and the Beatles *White Album*.

As for the high strangeness and alien abductions or reunions, Ernie said that if this happened and I had some recollection, why didn't I tell him about it at the time? Good question. Part of the reason is that my memories were somewhat muddled and fuzzy at the time. Also, I didn't tell him that I was psychic or had seen angels or read cards through telepathy with my mom or heard a dead man talk to me at an open casket funeral in Ballard either. So, maybe it isn't that unusual that I wouldn't share some of what I suspected had happened the first night of our road trip. He wouldn't have believed me then and probably doesn't believe me now. On the other hand, his memory could have been screened as effectively as mine was for over 40 years. Ernie said that he is agnostic about the paranormal. Did all this happen? I think it did, but Ernie wasn't so sure.

In an email, he mentioned that Occam's razor should be applied in determining what happened on the first night of the trip. Occam's razor is a principle from philosophy which states that given two explanations for the same event, the explanation that requires the least speculation is usually the better. In other words, the more assumptions you make, the more unlikely the explanation. Interestingly, in his last email to me, Ernie wrote: "What if I want to put *my* alien abduction experience into *my own* book? It's kind of spoiled if you publish it first. Anyway, I actually do remember some details. In particular, I remember pretending to be drugged or out but hearing the following snippet of conversation. I used to think this was from a dream but maybe it was real. *'Where'd you find this guy? He's a bit of a squealer, eh?'* said the first alien. *'You'd think they'd never seen pincers before,'* said the second alien. Then everything went black again, oh well. Maybe I'll remember more of this later." I wasn't sure if Ernie was joking or serious. Then he wrote in reference to my mentioning that I didn't want to do bad things and wanted to be good: "… what 'bad things' might we be talking about? Hmmm, maybe this is referring to the time you stood by and did nothing to help while the aliens were performing god-knows-what experiments on your friend. Naturally you have been racked by guilt and uncertainty ever since." Was he still kidding around, or was he angry? I'm not sure, and he hasn't returned my emails since. So, my dear readers, where does that leave us?

I did some research after the hypnosis session and my contact with Ernie through email and by telephone. In some old papers of mine, I found this poem that I had written not long after Ernie and I returned from our trip in 1977. It chilled me to the bone, especially the reference to pincers as Ernie had mentioned. I got very emotional reading it. I think it provides some validation for my strange experiences.

Visitors (1977)

Roll out the red carpet
And fill the toasts to brimming
We have visitors
As hosts, I think we're winning
They're a different breed
So, don't be shocked
At their hideous faces
They'll know their places
Here they are:
Good day sir,
How do you do?
"Die human die."
We were wrong
They stabbed our backs
They have control now
I sold out to the aliens
I'm sorry sirs
But I had to do it
I sold out
Past events are blurs
They had my family
Under steel pincers
They're mean
Can't you understand?

Rescue Operation (1978)

Around midnight on June 29, 1978, I was lying on a filthy, bare mattress in my brother's garage with a rusty hunting knife in my hand. Shaking and crying uncontrollably, the only question on my mind was whether I should slit my throat or stick the knife under my ribs and into my heart. Why was I ready to end my life? Simple answer, I just wanted the pain to stop. How did I get to that point? Well, my dear readers, that is quite a story.

June of 1978 in Seattle was typical: a little rain, a little wind, warm, and cool. Everyone who has lived in Seattle knows that the really good weather is in August (during Sea Fair) and in September. Early in June, the Seattle Supersonics had narrowly lost to the Washington Bullets in the NBA championship series. The musical film *Grease* had just premiered on June 13th, and the TV actor Bob Crane (who played Colonel Hogan on *Hogan's Heroes*) was brutally murdered on June 29. All these things may have concerned me, but not as much as my own inner turmoil.

When is a demonic experience not really a demonic experience? Answer: When it is both a demonic and alien experience. I decided to revisit my demonic encounter from the summer of 1978 documented in my first *Timeless* book as the story "Hell is Empty." In that story, I got a few things wrong. First, I had this demonic confrontation after I returned from Alaska, not before. And second, the trigger for the event was my attempt at suicide. That was something that I had conveniently forgotten. For this story, I had the help of hypnotherapist Yvonne Smith. I always knew that there was something untold about this frightful event in 1978, but it wasn't until now that I could face the truth.

I returned from Alaska on May 31, 1978. I had learned a lot from my short time working in Bristol Bay in the little town of South Naknek, but I came back too early. I had agreed to stay until the fall. My dad got me the job at Kenai Packers because he knew the Norwegian man named Ole, who ran the operation. In late May, when I told Ole that I had to return to Seattle early, he was furious. Ole called my father and vented his frustration and anger on him. My dad was embarrassed and then got angry at me. Dad had built me a special toolbox and gave me tools too. It doesn't seem like a big thing, but the act of giving me some of his carpenter tools was part of passing on his legacy. At the time, I didn't understand the value he placed on this gesture. My parents were renting out their house and heading to Norway. By getting the job in Alaska for the summer, they knew I'd have a place to live and a way to make a living. The plan fell apart when I returned early. I was embarrassed and had disappointed my father greatly. They were already disappointed because I had dropped out of the University of Washington after failing most of my classes. I had been wasting my time and their money. I knew how upset they were, and it was eating me up inside.

Because my parents had rented out the house, I moved into my brother's garage. Not long after I returned from Alaska, my brother helped me get a job with his friend who worked as a carpenter doing home remodeling. I worked for him for a while, and then quit. He got angry and took it out on my brother. Now my brother was mad at me too. I was living in his garage, sleeping on a bare mattress, and had no job, and no prospects. As the icing on this pathetic cake of despair, I was constantly fighting with my girlfriend Marianne. I was jealous all the time, was mean to her, pushed her around, and bullied her. I was so ashamed of myself and disappointed her as well.

So, back to that fateful night, June 29, 1978, I felt very alone; it was the loneliest time of my life. I knew I wasn't going to make it with my girlfriend, and I was certain that she was ready to dump me. I was mean and she deserved somebody nice. I was lost, disappointed with myself, drifting, and unsure of what was going to happen. I was in my Macbeth moment of "to be or not to be." I now understand what people who attempt and commit suicide are going through. It's often the pain that we can't see that will do them in. I know their pain. I just wanted the pain to stop for me. I was afraid, and hesitated, and I thought to myself that maybe I was going to fail at killing myself too. What a loser. Further disappointment. I looked around the garage and saw all the coffee cans filled with nails and screws, the boxes, the scrap lumber, old car parts, and the smell of oil and sawdust. It was a musty, dusty smell. It was dark outside and nearly midnight. At the moment I decided to go through with my suicide and was ready with the knife tip on my stomach, a column of fire erupted from the concrete floor in the garage. I was lying on my back on my mattress and couldn't move, as if I were paralyzed.

In the "Hell is Empty" story from the first *Timeless* book, I go into detail about that experience of the column of fire which I took to be demonic, but during hypnotherapy, I remembered much more. Under hypnosis, I began describing that night to Yvonne.

"Weird, I see stars, an open sky, even though there is a roof on the garage. There is purple, almost like clouds, wisping around, and an infinite number of stars," I said. Yvonne told me to use my body memory. I remembered that I felt something odd, like there was something wrong with my body, like a Charlie horse with my whole body, starting in my legs, I couldn't move them, it was hard to move my arms too.

"I feel like I'm very light, seeing stars, violet light fog or wispiness. The light is in front of me and all around me. I don't feel the mattress anymore, like on a cushion of air, angular lights, like in crosshatch pattern, it's a circuit board superimposed on a field of stars," I said. Yvonne urged me to remember the detail of the circuit board so I could draw it later.

"Dark, circuit board, little connections, purple lights all around me, movement in the background, black shadows, above me and moving left to right," I added. There was a continuous movement with the black shadows, and occasionally, there were blue flashes in the purple.

"I don't smell the dusty garage, very clean smell now," I said. I was now inside of a tube, not moving. I seemed to be silvery, me but a silvery version of me, in a tube. The tube is surrounding me, not much wider than me, so that I can move through easily. It's not made of glass or steel; it's made of particles, like so many grains of sand. I still see the purple and blue lights, and a field of stars behind that. Yvonne asked me if I heard any sounds?

"Roaring sound, hard to describe, it's not a column of fire, they're particles of different colors—blue, green, purple, orange, red, yellow. A lot of movement and the sound is coming from where the particle tube is being drawn to," I said. I was a little confused as to where I was.

"I'm still seeing a field of stars, green colors joining blue and the purple. It feels like there is no bottom and no top. I don't have a reference point. I'm suspended," I said.

The shadows stopped for a while, and things were calmer. Then, there were bigger, darker shadows, and smaller things were moving around.

"Not like shadows, they're like outlines. Occasionally I see an eye, in front of me, over me, a dark eye, it appears, then goes away," I said. I thought for a moment and was upset.

"Why do they scare me like that? The shadow people with the dark eyes…why have the gravelly, deep, scary voice, why make me think it was fire?" I was referring to my memory documented in "Hell is Empty."

"I don't see fire at all, it's all blue, purple, and black," I added.

Yvonne asked me if the beings in the shadows with the large dark eyes communicated with me.

"Communication? What I remember and see now is different than what I thought it was before. It's disconcerting," I said. "A name, they gave me a name, identified me. I was hearing what was being said, but not seeing them talk, or where it is coming from, it just comes to me. I don't know what is up and down, left and right. Still smells clean, I know I'm not in the garage."

Yvonne asked me to describe my surroundings.

"Very hard to say what is around me. No, not in a tube, I see hands, long fingers, over my chest or stomach, reaching for me, two of them, four more, coming back, it's dark because my eyes are closed. I don't know if I want to open my eyes," I said.

Yvonne reminded me that I was safe and in a safe place now.

"Rotating disc above me, bluish-purple light, shadowy figures around me, asking me if I'm okay. I say I don't know, I think so," I said.

Yvonne asked me how many figures I see.

"I can see a shadow figure on each side, at my feet, and by my head, so four at least," I said, then paused.

"Almost like I'm at the bottom of a well looking up at them, feeling like I can't move. Large dark eyes, blueish tinged heads, four of them, moving around me. Gravity isn't applying here. They seem to be floating too, but I feel like I'm floating in a shallow well, enclosed, it's cold, and very clean, a metallic clean, not like cleaning products, just pure and clean, an unnaturally clean smell," I said. There was a long pause, then Yvonne asked if I was still lying on my back.

"I sense that I'm in a fetal position, and I see things that look like lightning...like those globes that have electricity in them. It's around me, electrical flashes around me, almost like I'm inside of my own eye," I blinked hard as I thought of the view from the interior of my eye.

"There is this a round disc above me, it moves like it's a ceiling, but I can see through it. It seems to be part of where we are, a structure, or a force that is suspending me and us, because they're in the same space I am," I said.

Yvonne asked me what else I see around me.

"Little cylinders, like scuba tanks, around me, horizontal, whitish, off-white, in bundles, not one by one by one, but bundles. Everything is more open now, not enclosed, triangular shadows are moving around, and somebody is by my feet," I said. The shock of remembering all of this was beginning to set in a bit.

"I'm pointing down with my head, on my back again. Now I start to see purple and blue giving way to orangish-yellow," I said.

Yvonne asked me where I see these colors.

"This is up above me and moving down toward my feet. I have a feeling of dropping, falling, slowly, yellow, red, and orange taking over blue and purple, and moving downward," I said, and then paused as I shift my position on the couch.

"More natural colors, and the surroundings, they're more familiar. Everything is moving away from me now. I'm back on the mattress. Yes, in the garage again, but confused. It's dark, and I feel very alone again. There are more normal smells now…the dusty, dirty, oily, metal, sawdust smell of the garage," I added. Yvonne brought me out of my hypnotic state, and I was back on her couch and relaxed, although it took me a little while to open my eyes.

I had been hypnotized once before by Yvonne, but it felt deeper the second time. I knew the process better. I told Yvonne that what I was describing under hypnosis was kind of shocking because it was totally different than my conscious memory. It seemed to be a very different storyline. My previous memory, demonic in nature, was much more frightening than what I remembered under hypnosis. The hypnotic regression memory wasn't frightening. What I described in my story "Hell is Empty" was different than what I remembered under hypnosis. Could it be some combination of both memories? Was the column of fire from my story the tube that I described during my hypnosis session? Then it came to me in a sudden flash of comprehension.

"I feel like it was a rescue operation," I told Yvonne.

She asked if it was a rescue for me.

"Yes, for me. I was at a very low point in my life; that is why it was a rescue operation; suicide was on my mind," I told Yvonne.

The next night after my session with Yvonne, I remembered that I was in the process of killing myself with a knife in June 1978. That was a memory that was blocked by the aliens. A few days later, I illustrated what I remembered from the hypnosis session and from the dreams and visions I had for the two nights and days after. I also asked my spirit guides. I asked Anzar in particular.

"It was a big session. Are my illustrations accurate? What is your opinion? My other spirit guides as well, what do you think?" I asked.

"It is what I have said before, you are a hybrid," said Anzar.

"So, the experience in my brother's garage was both demonic and alien, like you said?" I asked.

"Demonic in the sense that it was presented as such in your memories, now you know it was also of alien origin," he said.

"So, I was in a tube of some sort? I asked.

"Yes. Processed as a hybrid. Your mom was too. So forth and so on," said Anzar.

"Whatever you guys can do to help me understand this experience and write about it, would be appreciated," I said. I also wanted to ask my dear departed friend Gene as well.

"Gene, what do you think?"

"Yes, it was, you got it, now onward! Move through it. We're a team," he said.

"Yeah, I can't do it without you, my friend. All of you," I said and was satisfied with the spiritual validation I received.

Research done at Harvard University shows that nine out of ten people who attempt suicide and survive will not die by suicide later. This is well documented in the literature about suicide. Suicidal crises tend to be rather short-lived. I've read that the few Golden Gate Bridge jumpers who survived knew immediately after they let go of the bridge rail that they had made the worst mistake of their lives and wanted another chance at life. So, did the aliens save me from the demons and suicide? I believe so. It was, indeed, a rescue mission, and maybe the aliens aren't so bad after all. This poem that I wrote in 1994 about the Vietnam War, oddly enough, may also help explain my despair in 1978, and the plight of abductees. Our lives are important, and we all have a mission on this Earth. As Leon, a Yakama medicine man, told me from the spirit world (see "Treetop Warriors" in the first *Timeless* book): "Always approach everything with love, guidance from the Creator is the love we feel."

Letter from Home (1994)

Don't write home
the lights are out
Grass grows tall
the fence has fallen
Sidewalks buckle
mailboxes crushed
Thinking is all too much
feeding is easier
The TV is on
but no one sees the truth
Don't write home
the dog has let himself out
The Plymouth has flats
the mower is rusted
The teapot is whistling
it'll dry itself trying
The TV is on
but no one hears what is said
Don't write home
the mail's stopped coming

The words melt together
their meaning glossy-smooth
Memories are now reality
heart, mind, and touch
Home is not the same
shadows move in opposite directions
Coming back to find yourself in the World
and no one will find you

Snake Eyes (1979)

American Express was my bank when I was stationed in West Germany from 1979 to 1981. We had a branch office on Coleman Barracks in Mannheim. It seemed like every time I went to the bank, Abby would be the teller I dealt with. She was a young Hispanic girl, pretty, with long black shiny hair, deep brown eyes, and an engaging smile. I was always friendly with her, and she reciprocated. It wasn't long until her friendliness seemed to cross a line into the realm of flirting. Don't get me wrong, I didn't mind at all, I mean, she was beautiful, but it just seemed odd. I was dating Anna who would become my wife, but that didn't seem to stop me from flirting with Abby every time I went to the bank.

One day, when I dropped by the American Express bank to cash a check, Abby noticed my prison guard uniform.

"Do you like working at the prison?" she said.

"Yeah, no, I don't know," I said.

"My husband works there too," she said. My heart sank. I thought she was interested in me and, without really thinking about it, I was playing the field and hoping Abby and I could get together.

"Oh, what's his name?" I asked.

"Specialist Walker," she said. I knew him, but he was in another guard platoon.

"Cool," I said, faking that I wasn't impacted by this news.

"You and Anna should come by some time for dinner," she said. I was floored. Did she know my girlfriend too? That was weird. Why had she been flirting with me then?

"Okay," I said, again not revealing my feelings of astonishment and disappointment. Girls always seem much smarter and more sophisticated than boys.

As fate would have it, Specialist Walker transferred to my guard platoon. Soon after that, we struck up a friendship, and he brought up his wife's offer again.

"You guys should come by for dinner," he said.

"Yeah, okay," I said.

"How about after our shift tomorrow?"

"Alright." I had to ask Anna, of course, but I knew she would be okay with going. I was still trying to figure out why Abby was so flirty with me when she knew I was dating Anna and I knew she was married to one of my fellow guards.

I had been dabbling with the study of magic ever since I met Anna in July of 1979. We then had a few weird experiences in the barracks (see my story "That Old Black Magic" in the first *Timeless* book). It appeared that the study of ritual magic tended to attract dark forces, something that I wasn't entirely aware of at that time. I had mentioned my interest in magic to Specialist Walker during our long shifts in the prison. He seemed genuinely interested, but not overly impressed or enthusiastic. The more I worked with him, the more I noticed that Specialist Walker had an unusual look. He usually wore glasses that grew darker in the light, transitional lenses. Behind the dark glasses, it seemed like he had squinty eyes and didn't ever look you in the eye when you spoke to him. He had a shock of blonde hair that swept across his forehead. He was skinny and of medium height. He was rather quiet, and when he did speak, it was in a monotone voice. He was smart and was always reading whenever he had a chance. One night, we were covering C-Block on a midnight shift in August 1979.

I had just completed my check of the cells and signed the appropriate suicide watch blocks on the clipboards that hung on the wall opposite each cell. Specialist Walker was reading the *Stars and Stripes* newspaper with his boots up on the desk.

"Everyone's breathing," I said.

"That's a relief," he said.

"Yeah, no extra paperwork, right?" I said, and laughed. He didn't respond and kept reading, his head buried behind the paper.

"I had a weird experience the other day," I said, referring to the demon head incident in Anna's barracks room. Still no reaction from Specialist Walker. A minute went by.

"You guys coming over or what," he said, finally, and still hiding behind the paper.

"Yeah, sure, maybe Friday," I said.

"Good," he said. I was picking up a strange vibe, and the hairs on the back of my neck stood up.

"We can talk about magic and stuff, your wife said she is interested in that," I said. Slowly, Specialist Walker lowered the newspaper and stared at me directly. He had taken off his glasses, and his eyes were not squinty and were wide open. They were also utterly black except for a narrow vertical slit! He had black, piercing, evil snake-like eyes that froze me in place and time. I was so frightened that I couldn't speak or breathe or move.

"Black magic," he said as he stared intently at me. Then, he brought the newspaper back up to cover his face. As soon as he hid again behind the paper, I was able to move, breathe, and speak. My body was adrenalized, and my heart racing, but I didn't want him to see that I was freaking out.

75

"Okay, but I'm not really into that kind," I said meekly. I was trying to figure out what had just happened. I had never seen anyone with black snake eyes like that. Because Walker wore dark glasses and was so squinty and never looked at people, I hadn't noticed.

Recently, I've read about black-eyed children. These mysterious creatures resemble kids from 10 to 14 years old. Reports are that they only appear at night and ask unsuspecting people to let them in their homes or cars with the pretense of needing a ride, to make a phone call, or get something to eat or drink. Some people think they might be vampires; others believe they are extraterrestrials, inter-dimensional beings, or demons. Upon seeing these children, people report feeling overwhelming fear and dread and escape in any way they can or immediately close the door. According to the website Snopes, the legend may have started with a post to a ghost-related mailing list by Brian Bethel in 1998. Many people have since reported incidents and even terrible things that happen after you let them in, but as far as I know, there is no documented proof. In this case, Specialist Walker was an adult, not a child, and what I'm writing about took place in 1979.

The next Friday after Specialist Walker revealed his secret, Anna and I drove to their house, which was a few kilometers away from the prison in Mannheim. It was a nice German home with a BMW parked in front and a beautiful garden with flowers. My first thought was how did they afford all this on a soldier's salary?

"She works too," Anna said, reading my mind. They welcomed us at the door and were very pleasant, and we had a lovely meal. At the time, I would drink occasionally, and they offered us lots of German wine before, during, and after our meal. Abby was not flirting with me, and all seemed somewhat normal.

I kept trying to look carefully at Walker's eyes, but I didn't notice anything unusual. The conversation was kept light, and the wine flowed freely. It wasn't long before both Anna and I were quite drunk. I didn't notice that Walker or Abby felt the effects of the alcohol. From that point on, my recollections are hazy at best. Did we pass out? Was I lying down in bed with Abby? Did Anna disappear for a while? I can't be sure.

The next thing I know, Anna and I are driving back to the barracks where we still lived in separate rooms. I don't remember feeling drunk, just confused. What had happened? Oddly enough, Specialist Walker didn't talk to me much after this dinner party, and neither did Abby when I did my banking. She almost acted like she didn't know me. About two months later, they were both gone. Where did they go? Who were they? What really happened? I don't know. Those black snake eyes still haunt me.

Tiger the Magic Cat (1980)

I love cats, and they love me. I have a special connection to them, and strange cats often come up to me to be petted. Cats have been part of my life since I was born. They say that there are cat people and dog people. A survey by the American Veterinary Medical Association revealed that 37 percent of American households had dogs, and 30 percent had cats. A survey from the University of Texas at Austin conducted by Dr. Sam Gosling found that dog people are 15 percent more extroverted than cat people, but cat people are 11 percent more open, meaning unconventional in their thinking. Interesting. Also revealing was data that showed cat people to be 12 percent more neurotic than dog people. There is also more hatred for cats than for dogs. Nearly 15 percent of those surveyed said they hated cats whereas only 2 percent said they hated dogs. I guess I'm more of a cat person, an unconventional, persecuted, neurotic, introverted, cat person. Try putting that on your resume. In truth, I love all animals including dogs, birds, porcupines, rabbits, and more. Snakes I can do without, but I don't necessarily hate them, like Indiana Jones.

I believe that the people who abhor cats are afraid of them. I think it's because they associate them with evil and feel they're untrustworthy. As I often tell my students, the basic difference between cats and dogs is that dogs will go to war with us, and cats won't. Although, what if cats could be trained for war? Imagine, if you will, 10,000 wild cats descending at 30 miles per hour on your fighting position, hissing, leaping through the air from all directions with needle-sharp claws and teeth. Scary. I think that the fear of cats is unjustified, but I'm aware that cats are generally associated with the paranormal, the supernatural, and the occult.

Some say that witches use cats to practice their witchcraft. Such cats are known as familiars. Supposedly, the witch and the cat are drawn to each other to form a lifetime alliance. Because cats can be somewhat aloof and mysterious, they have been associated with the occult throughout history. Cats were worshipped as gods in ancient Egypt and even mummified. These Egyptian cat deities helped spread the magical mystique of cats, which led to them being seen as supernatural creatures. According to witches, they believe you can learn more magic from a cat than you can another witch. In other words, a cat won't turn you into a toad just for asking the wrong question. Supposedly, cats can also chase away evil spirits. I can attest to that. I slept best with my cat next to me knowing that he could see evil entities quicker than I could and would warn me. Witches feel that cats can help guide them between the world of the living and the world of the dead. I've read that cats are the only domestic animal not mentioned in the Bible. I wonder why?

Studies have shown that dogs were domesticated long before cats. Maybe cats aren't really domesticated. *Felis catus* isn't that different than its wild version *Felis silvestris*. Many scientists believe cats are only semi-domesticated, unlike dogs who need us and would likely die if left on their own. Egyptians, of course, were crazy about cats, but the domestication of cats may have begun in Cyprus nearly 9000 years ago. Some believe that cats are self-domesticated. In other words, they have chosen to domesticate themselves as it suits them. How clever of them. They still retain all their hunting skills even if they are well-fed. Dogs have been much more selectively bred than cats as there are 400 breeds of dog to only 45 cat breeds.

I've had many cats in my life starting with Smokie, who guarded me in my crib. My mom said that Smokie, a light grey long-haired cat, would hiss at anyone who came near me. Then there was Ralphie; he was a big, short-haired, black and white tomcat. He protected me in 1964, detailed in my story "Big Bad John" in this book. He was put down after he developed distemper and attacked me, gashing my forehead with his claws.

"He didn't mean to do it...he was sick!" I remember pleading with my parents. My protest fell on deaf ears, so on a dreary rainy day, I went with my sister and her husband Terje to the vet's office in Seattle to put an end to Ralphie's life. Terje took a struggling Ralphie wrapped in a blanket into the vet's office at the back of a drab old building. I cried and cried as I waited in the car, staring out the back passenger side window through the raindrops.

Red and Sis came next. They were orange kitties that I found abandoned at one of the apartment buildings my dad built in Bothell, Washington. They didn't last very long, Red went first, the victim of a coyote attack, then Sis got very sick and died. I remember telling my mom that I couldn't handle losing any more pets. That sad realization about losing my beloved pets led to a serious discussion about losing members of my family. My mom said to me that our loved ones were in heaven.

"My kitties too?" I asked.

"Yes," said mom. I was still heartbroken.

Tiger, a grey, black, white, and orange tabby cat, came into my life in 1969. He was my friend, my constant companion, and he loved me no matter what. Tiger was born in Ballard, Washington, and lived with my sister and her first husband Terje in an apartment not far from where my parents and my sister lived when they came to America in 1948.

One of Tiger's favorite games was catch. On lazy summer days, he would lay on the sundeck in front of our house, close to the railing, with his paws hanging over. He would meow to get my attention, and I would get a tennis ball. He would watch me carefully as I positioned myself below him, turning his head playfully sideways, and then I would throw the tennis ball straight up to him. Tiger would catch the ball with his claws, then release it back to me.

"Yeah, Tiger, good kitty, kitty," I would say. We would do this for several minutes. We both enjoyed the game and each other's company.

In our kitchen, we would all eat at the breakfast bar sitting on tall rotating chairs. Tiger was always there at our feet looking for handouts. His favorite food was bacon, so he was always early for breakfast. If you didn't give him a piece of bacon fast enough, he would remind you by sticking his claws in your leg. Ouch! If the bacon was too hot, he would circle it, taking little nips at it until it was cool enough. Anytime you used the can opener, he came running. He also came running if he heard me pouring cereal in a bowl. He loved ice cream, and I would always let him lick my bowl clean. What a pal!

When we had guests, Tiger would always come out to greet them and make passes at the coffee table with his strategically hooked tail, dipping it in whatever food was near the edge, hoping it would be given to him. He didn't like it when one of my mom and dad's friends came over with her little chihuahua named DeeDee. Tiger would make an appearance for the carefully defined purpose of making the little dog go crazy. He would then exit with a slow nonchalant walk as if he had no idea what the ruckus was about in the living room. Then he would come back from a different direction, and again the dog would go nuts furiously barking, frothing at the mouth, and snapping with its eyes bulging out. I thought DeeDee would have a heart attack. Tiger was such a prankster.

Tiger kept me safe and protected me. I liked to get under a blanket over the heat register on the floor in our living room in the wintertime. Tiger would join me, and we would get nice and toasty. I called this a heat blanket, but maybe it was our version of a sweat lodge. When I was home alone for the first time at age 12, he helped me. From our house on the hill, I remember crying and staring at 55th avenue below through our big picture window, hoping that each set of car lights that approached would be Mom and Dad returning. I was afraid of every little noise in the house. Were monsters coming? Aliens? Demons? Tiger kept me company, lying next to me on the couch. Eventually, I feel asleep on the couch, and then Tiger thought it would be a good time to sneak into the kitchen to try to steal some food on the counter. He accidentally knocked over some pots and pans that crashed to the floor waking me up and scaring me almost to death. I knew he was sorry, both that he scared me and that he got caught.

Tiger used to get under my mom's feet in the kitchen, which would cause her to yell in old northern Norwegian dialect: *Nei, nu må du gå unna skanken* (No, now you have to get out from under my feet). Every time my mom was cooking, there was Tiger under her feet and nearly tripping her. She would sometimes throw him outside and other times, just laugh. Tiger had a darker side too. I brought home a kitten in 1970 because I thought Tiger needed a companion. He was a black and white long hair cat that mom named *Svarte Per* (Black Pierre). Tiger and Svarte Per got along because the newcomer didn't challenge the top cat. Svarte Per had a tiny little meow, like a kitten, but when he was mad, he sounded like a mountain lion. Tiger was usually nice to Svarte Per, but he had an odd habit. It would usually begin with Svarte Per minding his own business, lazily lying on the rug or chair when Tiger would approach and lie

84

down peacefully next to him. Then Tiger would start cleaning his buddy. Very sweet. After a few minutes, Tiger would stop cleaning, look around, and with sudden aggression, attack Svarte Per as the fur would fly. Mom would then throw them both out. Poor Svarte Per.

When I got out of the US Army in 1981, we moved to Butte, Montana. I eventually failed in engineering school, and then we moved to Minneapolis, Minnesota. It was there that my wife Anna rescued a kitten who was about to be drowned in the Mississippi River. We named him Puff. He was a very light orange color, like a Creamsicle. Puff the Magic Fleabag was his full name. He stayed with us when I re-entered the service and we moved to Alabama and on to North Carolina, then Salinas, California, and eventually back to Seattle in 1986. We bought a house in Everett, Washington, in 1986, and Puff enjoyed having his own home and a large vacant lot behind us where he could hunt for mice. My two eldest sons, Bjørn and Byron, loved that cat. Sadly, one day he disappeared and never came back. We briefly had a rescue cat named Baby, so named because she cried all the time and wanted to be snuggled. She was a grey tabby with an unfortunate goiter under her neck. We went on vacation and the old neighbors had her put down while we were gone because they thought she was suffering. More sadness.

In 1990, we sold our house and moved to Bowling Green, Ohio, so that I could start my history doctoral program. We quickly adopted two cats—Fifi and Norton. Fifi was a beautiful calico long-haired cat, and Norton was a short-haired, orange tabby. Norton was the only cat that I was allergic to for some reason. He always made me sneeze. Fifi was a beautiful cat, very friendly, and she loved plain donuts. When Anna and I were divorced, I lived nearby, and when the kids came over for visitation, Fifi would come over as well. She was a great cat. Norton didn't last long, unfortunately. He ran away.

The next cat that came into my life was Malcolm. He was a white and black short-haired cat who had been an old street-fighting alley cat in Burien, Washington. His ears were both chewed up, and he had a crooked, broken tail. When I visited the vet's office, I immediately noticed him and felt compelled to reach into his cage and pet him. My friend, who worked there, cautioned me.

"He is feral and will bite you!" Malcolm didn't bite me; he nuzzled my hand gently and sweetly. He chose me, and I chose him. Malcolm loved sleeping on a shelf I positioned on the old steam radiator. His fur would get so hot that it hurt to touch him. Malcolm loved being warm probably because he had spent so many nights out in the cold and wet Pacific Northwest weather. I cared for him until 1998 when he succumbed to feline AIDS. Heartbreaking. Sofia came next— she was a wild barn cat from Bowling Green, Ohio. She was probably the feistiest cat I've ever owned. Sofia would pee on anything left on the floor, towels, clothes, whatever. She was also quick to challenge anyone, human or animal, to a fight. Sofia moved with us from Bowling Green to Seattle to Southern California. One day Sofia decided to move in with the neighbors, and that was it. She was tired of us and chose someone else. Hilarious.

But of all the cats I've had, Tiger was the most special of all. Tiger lived for 11 years. When I was in school, Tiger would meet me at the bottom of our hill where the school bus dropped me off and then walk up the long driveway with me. He had a pretty big area of operation. Unfortunately, Tiger loved to play chicken with cars that drove up our long steep driveway—just like a dog. I think he was part dog. As he grew older, he slowed down and had developed a pot belly, so his silly antics had become life-threatening. He always scared my mom when she drove up the driveway.

"Å Herre Gud, nå må du gi deg," she said in Norwegian. (No, oh my god, now you have to stop it). In 1980, while I was stationed in West Germany, Tiger was accidentally run over by my father. Dad was coming home from work, and as he drove up the driveway, he didn't see Tiger and the old boy slipped under the truck tires. That was it. No one was more heartbroken than my dad. Mom said that he made a custom-built coffin for Tiger and buried him in the backyard by an old stump under some huckleberry bushes, his favorite spot.

So, was Tiger magical? Hell yes! He allowed himself to be my pet, under his rules, and he did whatever he wanted to do, even if he was more like a dog than a cat. Tiger was a rugged individualist. The ideal American. He helped guide my vision of the mystical and the connection between animal and human spirits. Tiger could be playful, and he could be vindictive. He could be loving, and he could be a skilled hunter. Tiger understood me, and I understood him. He was more than a friend; he was a mentor. When he slept by my pillow at night, I knew I was safe and that no harm would come to me. He tried to warn me when I was contacted and taken by extra-terrestrials in 1973. Tiger's antics would make my mom and dad smile and laugh, and I know that was good because my parents had many sorrows and hardships in their lives. His death made us all cry. I tried to emulate his catlike style when I was younger. He is partially responsible for me accepting my paranormal abilities. Tiger showed me the meaning of true friendship and helped me to grow up and learn to deal with profound loss. If that isn't magical, I don't know what is.

I Like Big Butte (1982)

You might wonder why I moved my family to Butte, Montana, in the middle of the winter in 1982. Well, it's a good question, and I'll tell you. I'd just been discharged from the army in November 1981, and the military returned us to my place of enlistment–Seattle, Washington. We (my then-wife Anna and my two oldest boys, Bjørn and Byron), lived with my parents for a few weeks. I'd been away from home since 1978 and, as much as I loved my parents, it wasn't easy living at home again, especially with two kids. Byron was only one month old. My dream was to go back to college and get a degree in petroleum engineering and then get a job working on an oil platform off the coast of Norway. I wanted to make my father proud. I was accepted at Montana Tech (formerly Montana School of Mines) in Butte, Montana, a historic town that sits on the continental divide at an elevation of 5538 feet.

I drove out ahead to secure a place for us to live, and as I approached Butte, I saw Big Butte, the prominent volcanic mountain that looms over the city. I felt oddly attracted to this prominent geologic feature. I got a room at the City Center Motel, and I ate Thanksgiving dinner at Denny's nearby. In 1917, when copper was king, Butte was a city of nearly 100,000 inhabitants and thriving. "The richest hill on Earth," they called it. But those days were gone, and I could tell that the town was just a shell of what it had been with only 30,000 citizens remaining in 1981. There were abandoned mansions and buildings everywhere. I could see the remnants of headframes from old mineshafts, some as deep as 3800 feet underground. Butte was the hometown of Robert Craig Knievel, Jr., better known as Evel Knievel. He was a hero to my little friends and me in my old neighborhood. We used to build ramps so we could jump like him on our bikes. Evel

Knievel was a world-famous daredevil stunt performer and entertainer. During his illustrious career, he attempted more than 75 death-defying motorcycle jumps. They said he had broken every bone in his body, some of them twice. In 1974, he attempted to jump across the Snake River Canyon in Idaho in the Skycycle X-2 rocket, but the parachute deployed prematurely, and the stunt failed.

In the center of town was the Berkeley Pit, the world's largest open-pit copper mine—one mile wide and 1800 feet deep. The place I picked for us to live was a poor choice. It was above a garage and was way too small for a family of four. After a few extremely cold winter months, we moved to 221 North Jackson Street uptown Butte, less than a mile from the infamous Dumas Brothel and one mile away from the Berkeley Pit. It was an old house in a poor rundown neighborhood. The oil furnace was not working well, so we used a converted 55-gallon drum fireplace in the living room to provide enough heat. Our neighbors were extremely poor. They had six kids ranging in age from six to 18. Because I was in engineering school, they figured I was smart. Their eldest son had already dropped out of school. The mother was in her late thirties, pretty, but careworn. She was an alcoholic. Her husband only came around occasionally, when the welfare check came in. They would pile into his broken-down truck and head to town for a fancy meal to celebrate. After dinner, they would get drunk and her husband would hit her and leave. That was their cycle. Anna had asked her if we should call the police and she said no.

There is nothing romantic about poverty. It is brutal and ugly. There was dog crap on the floor of our neighbor's house, and the whole place was infested with fleas. They slept on bare mattresses. I felt rich and privileged compared to our neighbors, even though we were just living on my army college fund money

90

(about $600 per month). One day, the mother came over with her youngest son.

"Heard you could doctor, so we came over," said our raggedy neighbor lady. Her crooked smile revealed a few missing teeth. She had a shapely figure, and her greasy blonde hair hung around her shoulders, and her deep brown, squinted eyes and cragged charcoal-smudged face offered a glimpse of fading beauty.

"Benny here is needin' stitches out," she said as she exhaled her cigarette smoke to punctuate her words. I was in shock. Just then, Anna walked in with our boys.

"I'm just a college student, not a doctor," I said.

"The free clinic is too far and no car," she said. I paused to look at the kid.

"I don't know," I said. Anna started fixing something to eat for the boys.

"You a college boy, so we figured you's smart enough," she said. Anna laughed.

"He's smart enough, it'll be alright," Anna said. I looked at the boy's face. He had stitches above his right eyebrow. I nodded my head in agreement. After scrubbing my hands clean, I retrieved some xylocaine, cotton balls, alcohol, tweezers, and some tiny scissors from the bathroom medicine cabinet. I sterilized the tweezers and scissors with a lit match and then with alcohol. The neighbor lady lit another cigarette and walked over by the fridge.

"You mind if I grab a beer?" she asked.

"Help yourself," Anna said. She popped open the can of Coors and took a big gulp. Anna was feeding Byron in the highchair, and Bjørn was eating a sandwich watching me practice medicine without a license. After a few minutes, the procedure was done. I was able to get the stitches out. The barefoot, shirtless boy ran outside to play.

"Much obliged, sir," she said, gently brushing my hand and kissing me on the cheek.

"Cup of coffee?" I asked. She winked and smiled.

"Thanks, no. Another time. Old man's in from the mine, we're gettin' ready for dinner out," she said. She turned and left.

Later that evening there was a knock on the door. The little ragged neighbor boy who had the stitches was out of breath.

"Mom's hurt bad, come quick, sir!" I followed him and noticed his bare feet barely miss the broken bottles in their little yard. Their house reeked of dog crap and moldy old piss-soaked rugs. The paint was peeling inside and out. The heavy smell of cigarette smoke hung thick in the air. The teenage boy came out of their kitchen.

"Old man whooped her but good this time," he said. He showed me to the upstairs bedroom where his mom was lying on a filthy, bare mattress writhing in pain. Her face was swollen; she had bloody hands.

"She had too much to drink again," said the teenage boy.

"No, get out, the old man coming back," she said.

"I'll take you to a doctor," I said.

"No doctor, no cops, go, hurry, please," she said as she cried. I touched her hand and smiled, and then I glanced at the teenage boy.

"You come and get me if there's more trouble," I said.

92

"Don't call the cops, they'll split us up again," the boy said. As I left, the little boy lay down next to his mom and waved at me. His mournful glistening eyes told the story. I had this feeling that our old rental house had ghosts; I never felt alone even when I was alone. The spirits in that house seemed to be connected to all the other houses in the neighborhood. It was almost like the whole neighborhood was cursed. We all suffered from dysentery and some older folks died when the Berkeley Pit began to fill with water and poison our city water system. There was no mention in the newspaper. It was all word of mouth. Such was a day in the life in uptown Butte not far from the Berkeley Pit.

Butte was filled with ghosts. It was like a living ghost town because I think there were probably more ghosts than living people. In August 1917, International Workers of the World (IWW) organizer, Frank Little was killed by vigilantes. He was attempting to organize a strike by miners against the Anaconda Copper Mining Company. Six masked men dragged Frank out of his hotel room in Butte and hanged him over the Milwaukee Road trestle south of town.

One of my friends told me that the trestle was still there in 1981 and that devil worshippers use it to hold their evil black masses. We hiked through a thin crust of snow up from the road to the trestle to look for traces of devil worship. We found what looked like a fire pit but didn't find anything else. It did have a creepy feeling, though. Why did people have a fire up here? The wind was blowing, and eerie noises emanated from the trestle.

"Let's get out of here," I said. We hurried back to the car.

I wasn't successful in engineering school. I spent most of my time drawing and writing my comic strip *Snark* (now spelled with a C in the new comic book *Snarc*) for the *Technocrat* school newspaper. Often, I would hike up to the top of Big Butte to think. It was an excellent place to try to figure things out, and I felt energized standing at its 6299-foot peak. Big Butte is an inactive rhyolitic volcano. It is made of volcanic rocks that are 30-50 million years old. The old volcano sits on top of ancient granite or quartz monzonite that formed almost 80 million years ago and is the source of all the ore minerals that made Butte famous. Oddly, Big Butte is not a butte at all. A butte is defined as a small flat-topped hill created by erosion. Big Butte was buried in younger gravel material until an uplift of the Rocky Mountains, which brought it into view. If it weren't for the protective gravel, there would be no trace left of the inactive volcano.

In 1910, students from the Montana School of Mines (now known as Montana Tech), built the famous letter M on Big Butte. Residents consider the peak, the namesake of the town, to be a sentinel and feel a call to adventure when scaling Big Butte. During one of my climbs of Big Butte, I had an unusual experience. When I reached the summit, I could see the entire city and the valley sprawled out before me. To the East, I could see the majestic mountains that formed the continental divide. As I was enjoying the view, I began to slip into a trance-like state and heard a droning sound coming from a weirdly shaped boulder on the leeward side of the peak, perhaps twenty yards down. Upon further investigation, I found a black onyx stone, about the size of a baseball, tucked away in a small cave beneath the large boulder. It seemed to be glowing around its edges as it emitted a droning sound. I rubbed my eyes to make sure I didn't just see the sun's reflection or glare. I sat there for a few moments listening and staring until I felt a strange burning sensation between my ears. Then I heard a voice inside my head.

"This is portal number 307. Prepare for the arrival. Instructions are forthcoming," the voice said. Did I imagine that? I broke out of my trance-like state. What did this mean? Frightened, I put the black onyx rock back in the cave and headed down the mountain.

Although I wrote about this strange incident on Big Butte in my journal, I didn't give it more thought and tried to forget the bad luck that ensued for the rest of our time in Montana. Only recently, I did some research on the number 307 and found that there is an error code HTTP 307 Temporary Redirect status response in our computers that indicate a resource that was requested has been temporarily moved to a new location. In the year 307, Constantine was made Caesar and returned to Britain. Also known as Constantine the Great, he was the first Christian Roman emperor. The number 307 is a prime number meaning it is a natural number greater than (1) that has no positive divisors other than (1) and itself. The number 307 is also a Chen prime, meaning that p+2 is either another prime or a product of two prime numbers (2p+2). Chen primes are named after Chen Jingrun who in 1966 proved that there is an infinite number of such primes. If you take 307 as degrees on a compass, in the opposite direction (back azimuth), 127 degrees from Butte, Montana, you will cross through Yellowstone National Park in Wyoming. The area code for the entire state of Wyoming is 307. Interesting coincidence, I guess.

More importantly, I wondered about the idea of this stone being a portal. There is the Montana Vortex portal near Glacier National Park, but that was 232 miles north of Butte. I suppose a portal to other dimensions could appear anywhere. For instance, in this and my previous *Timeless* books, I've written about another portal on Valley Center Avenue near my home. The similarity between these two locations was that I was drawn to both of them.

Butte has other paranormal legends. I was told of the ghost of the headless co-ed at Montana Tech, who roamed the parking lots at midnight, but I never spotted her. There was also the haunted Dumas Brothel (also known as the Dumas Hotel) that only closed its doors in 1982, the same year I moved to Butte. The bordello opened in 1890 and was patronized by miners. It was the longest operating brothel in the United States. The Dumas is a two-story brick building that also includes a basement with secret underground tunnels for patrons. It is located on Mercury Street less than a mile from where I lived. The current owner, who offers tours, claims that several ghosts haunt the Dumas Hotel. The TV show *Ghost Adventures* visited the hotel and found evidence of spirits. I do remember walking by the Dumas one day and felt a strange vibration even from the outside. It's considered one of the most haunted locations in Butte. Visitors have seen the ghosts of prostitutes and their customers walking the halls. Photographs have revealed strange anomalies that many believe are images of the ghosts.

By most measures, living in Butte, Montana, was an unmitigated disaster. I only passed one class (chemistry) and failed calculus and technical writing (of all things). Our only vehicle broke down and my family, including a two-month-old boy and a two-year-old boy, had to walk everywhere we went. I remember using a little red wagon to carry our groceries home from the store. Our attempt to start a bar band failed miserably. We were short of money, and my temper was out of control. I was forced to enter the army again by joining the reserves to earn some extra money when I flunked out of Montana Tech. Despite these setbacks, I learned many valuable lessons while living in

Butte. I wasn't going to feel sorry for myself and let my family fall into the trap of poverty and despair, I wasn't going to take any more unnecessary risks, and I wasn't going to give in to the temptations of the dark side. Ultimately, I realized that I wasn't meant to be a soldier or an engineer in the fossil fuel industry and that I had a more artistic, creative, and paranormal future ahead of me. It has taken me quite a while to fully realize who I was and what I was supposed to do. Culminating with my experience on Big Butte, in retrospect, my future path was set in motion.

Beguiled and Bewitched (1999)

Have you ever done something and then almost immediately realized that you might have made the worst mistake of your life? Well, that's what this story is about, truly a cautionary tale. In the summer of 1999, my father was in the final stages of his battle with Alzheimer's and Parkinson's disease. It had come to the point where he couldn't live in the last of the many homes that he had built in Seattle. I found an assisted living residential home for him where he would be cared for day and night. He had his own room that was filled with as much of his own furniture as possible. I still remember dropping him off and helping him get settled into his new home. All went well until I had to leave, and dad went and got his jacket and hat.

"No, Dad, you're staying here," I said.

"This isn't my home," he said.

"This is your new home. You're staying with these nice people," I said. Dad just looked at me and then turned his head to the side before he faced me again, and I noticed a look that used to terrify me when I was a kid and still was unsettling to me as an adult.

"So, you're making the decisions now," he said with anger causing his voice to tremble. He slowly put his hat and jacket back in the coat closet and walked back to his room and closed the door. It broke my heart to see him resign himself to being left behind, no longer in charge of his own destiny. I cried as I drove away. How could I do this to my father?

Just before I left for Seattle from Los Angeles to make arrangements for my father, one of my former students from when I was teaching in Seattle (a woman who was three years older than me) had been flirting with me through email. I'll call her Beatrice. Each succeeding email was bolder than the last. She had been one of my online students several years before when I first started teaching after graduate school. I knew the rules, no fraternization with students. I should have discontinued the emails, but I didn't. I could blame it on the anguish I was feeling with my father's ill health, or the pressure I faced at work with two administrators who were trying to get me fired, but the truth was, I was weak, and my marriage was suffering. When I returned from Seattle, Beatrice propositioned me. She even sent me a picture of her and her wife (they were a lesbian couple). She was married, and so was I. My reaction to the proposition was shock at first, and then it intrigued me. My first mistake was not to nip this in the bud and politely decline her offer.

I returned to Seattle because my dad had run away from his assisted living home. The nurse in charge said that he had to be in an Alzheimer's lockdown unit. I found one for him, and it was awful. The facility smelled like urine and feces, a far cry from his residential assisted living home. It was there that I think my dad gave up. I went to visit him one day and he was catatonic. I had to lift him out of his bed like a baby and put him in a wheelchair. A few days later, he came down with a massive infection and the doctors said that he needed to be transferred to hospice care and didn't have long to live. It all happened so fast that my emotions didn't have time to catch up. I had to go back to California to finish up my class, so my sister and brother were in charge. I wasn't back for more than two days when I received a call from my dad's doctor.

"Your father refuses to eat or drink. Do you want us to insert a feeding tube?" he asked.

"Will he be able to recover if we do?" I asked.

"No, but it will keep him alive," he said.

"Will he be conscious and able to move around?" I asked.

"Not for long," he said. I thought long and hard. My dad was a strong, active, and proud man.

"What would you do if it was your father?" I asked. The doctor was caught off guard by my question. Almost a whole minute went by.

"I wouldn't do it," he said, with great emotion in his voice.

"No feeding tube," I said.

I booked another flight for Seattle and it was then that my former student called me in my office. She had tracked me down and was in Los Angeles.

"You want to meet?" she said.

"Sure, but I have to leave tomorrow," I said.

"Okay, how about five o'clock today?" she asked. I thought for a while.

"Okay, the Stater Brothers parking lot," I said. I felt like a horrible person already, and I hadn't even done anything yet. I met Beatrice at the appointed time, and we had sex in her van. I knew as soon as it started that it was a horrible mistake, but it was like I wasn't in my body, I was hovering over my body. I felt like she was in total control of me. I noticed that she kept whispering my name as we did the horrible and sordid act. I found it odd, but it didn't stop me. I was in tremendous mental pain and my judgment was clouded. From that point on, I was so emotionally numb that nothing mattered. When my father died on August 20, 1999, I was carrying on an affair with a married woman, myself also being married. That wasn't what my parents had taught me. Wrong seemed right, and right seemed wrong.

Over the course of the next few years, I tried breaking it off many times, but she stalked me, and I gave in because I was weak. I tried attending Sex Addicts Anonymous (SAA) meetings, but I would arrange for Beatrice to meet me after each meeting, and we'd have sex in my car. Classy, I know, but I couldn't stop myself. It was like a drug addiction. I would go on vacation with my family, and all I could think of was meeting up with her. I felt so ashamed of myself and the more ashamed and depressed I was, the more I would continue the affair seeking relief from the pain. It was as if I was under her spell. Beatrice mentioned that she had practiced witchcraft with some lesbian friends of hers, but I didn't ask too many questions. I should have explored that aspect of this relationship a bit more, but I was too focused on my next sexual fix. I felt dirty and was starting to become an accomplished liar as I told my wife that I was going for a run, or to the store, or into work, only to meet with this woman and have sex. I began to have panic attacks after the clandestine meetings. I knew it was wrong, but I couldn't stop.

In 2003, I was awarded a Fulbright Professor position in Norway. I was happy for several reasons. One, it was a very prestigious award, and only 600 professors are given this opportunity in the United States every year. Two, I would be able to focus on my family and my career and be away from Beatrice and my cheating. Three, because I was still being attacked by two administrators who were trying to fire me, I thought I might be able to parlay a permanent position teaching in Norway and get away from them and the constant threat of termination. A dream come true. I was able to break away from this woman during that six-month period. Unfortunately, our time in Norway was cut short because our renters were threatening to stop paying rent which would cause us not to be able to pay our mortgage. We were forced to return in December 2003, six months earlier than expected. I figured I could resist Beatrice when I returned to the

United States, but I was wrong. I went right back to sneaking and cheating more than ever before. I returned to counseling to see if that would help.

It was in San Diego in 2005 that I had an epiphany. I saw myself in a hotel room window reflection having sex with Beatrice, and I didn't recognize the man in the reflection. It was shocking. What had I become? I had never felt lower and more despicable. Beatrice had a traffic accident after one of our secret rendezvous. I took that as a sign that I should stop. It was around this time that my wife found an email from Beatrice that spoke of our affair. She kicked me out and my marriage was over. I never returned to Beatrice and when she found out that I had a relationship with another woman, she decided to strike out at me. She called my academic dean and told him what was going on and tried to get me fired.

"Did you sleep with her when she was your student?" my dean asked on the phone. I was mortified.

"No, it was after," I said, ashamed of myself to the core. "And it was when I was teaching up in Seattle, not here," I added.

"Okay," he said. I knew I was okay in terms of keeping my job, but I was terribly embarrassed.

"Out of curiosity, how old is she?" he asked.

"Three years older than me," I answered.

"Good. Yeah, not a legal problem, but certainly stupid, I must say," he said.

"I agree. I'm sorry that she got you involved," I said.

I know that all of this was my fault, and I can only blame myself. Excuses are not appropriate camouflage for bad behavior. However, I now know that she had been collecting my hair and other personal items and was casting spells on me to keep me with her. I caught her many times muttering something weird using my name when we were together. When I broke it off, she lowered the boom on me, and I suppose I deserved it. I had been beguiled and bewitched, yes, but I can only blame myself.

In the Kingdom of the SMuRfs (2008)

Why would a 50-year-old man who has been out of the service for 23 years suddenly join the military again? Well, that is an excellent question. First, let me clarify; I joined the California State Military Reserve (CSMR), which was quite different than the active military, or even the reserves or national guard. The story began in Fort Ord, California, in April 1986, when I left the US Army under somewhat unusual circumstances. Although my discharge was honorable and not "bad paper," I later felt guilty about not completing my mission. You see, I wanted to be a medical evacuation (medevac or dust-off) pilot when I rejoined the US Army in 1983. However, the army, an organization that never gives anybody what they want, put me in a combat arms unit—the 1/17th Air Cavalry, where I flew OH-58 (Bell 206 Jet Ranger) helicopters. Consequently, I decided to get out of the army and return to civilian life. So, in April 1986, I was honorably discharged from the military for failure to make permanent promotion (I left active duty as a Warrant Officer 1). Ironically, I was promoted to Chief Warrant Officer 2 in the inactive reserves in 1987. A few years later, I was finally relieved from all military obligations. I began to feel heavy remorse about my decision to leave the service as the Gulf War began, because my flight school buddies went to war, and I was safe at home.

I was in my doctoral program at Bowling Green State University during the Gulf War and finished in 1993. I moved back to Seattle, Washington, my hometown. While teaching part-time at Green River Community College in Auburn, Washington, and Pacific Lutheran University in Tacoma, Washington, I thought about re-joining the military. We had financial difficulties and unreliable health insurance. Because I was having recurring dreams of being in the military, I figured it must be fate, and who am I to deny my destiny foretold in my dreams? Focusing on remaining physically fit, I even went as far as to fill out a prior service packet and take the physical and Armed Services Vocational Aptitude Battery (ASVAB) test again in 1996. I can remember how weird it was to go down to the Armed Forces Entrance and Examination Station (AFEES, now known as Military Entrance Processing Station or MEPS) in Seattle, Washington. Was it a dream or reality? Was I really going to re-enter the army? When I left the service in 1986, I could never have imagined re-joining. But, as my friend and colleague, Dr. Dale Salwak, says, "every departure is prelude to an arrival."

I was twice as old as most of the folks at MEPS. As I was lined up with the kids for testing, one of the smart-ass sergeants at the station winked and said: "Hi grandpa, a little long in the tooth, aren't we?" He was right, of course. I ended up not joining because I was overweight. Thank God and Dolly Madison. In 2008, I began to realize that there were some problems I needed to tidy up in my life, and they weren't just financial. One of those things was to deal with the great remorse I felt about leaving the military. How could I get this haunting feeling off my mind? Then it dawned on me that joining the CSMR could help me deal with this sense of failure and the feeling of not completing my mission. I told my girlfriend Ginger (now my wife) that I would thrive in the military setting the CSMR provided. She wasn't convinced.

Armstrong, one of my Vietnam War history students at Citrus College, had told me about the CSMR in early 2008. I wasn't quite sure what to make of his story when he told me he had enlisted in the military. You see, although he was a great person, he had only one arm. I wanted to believe him, but I couldn't imagine the military accepting a man with one arm. Frankly, it was hard to believe that such an organization existed. I confirmed its existence with my friend Manny who is a counselor with the Veterans Administration (VA). Then I did some research online and sent off some emails to the CSMR recruiters in Southern California. After several email exchanges, I decided to attend one of their orientations.

I drove down to the National Guard Armory in Long Beach, California, on August 9, 2008. The orientation was to begin at 0900 military time (I've never converted). A few of the CSMR soldiers stood around the back door as I walked up. They were cheerful and friendly as they smoked cigarettes and talked. I noticed that some of them were wearing the new Army Combat Uniform (ACU). It was hard to tell a person's rank with these new uniforms. At first, it felt bizarre to be around military people again. Then this strangeness turned to an odd familiarity. All of this made for a sense of apprehension and excitement as I entered the building. I found the briefing room and sat down at a long table and began to look at the recruits around me—what a bizarre collection of folks. They looked like an unholy assembly of gun show enthusiasts, science fiction conventioneers, and shopping mall security cops. Just as I began to critically appraise the "type" of person who wanted to join the CSMR, I remembered that these were fellow recruits, and I wasn't an omniscient observer. Genius at work—pure genius on my part.

One man stood out. His name was Eugene, and he was of medium height and build and had black hair that looked "re-touched." I figured he was about 45 years old. Eugene sat in front of a pile of paperwork and folders at least 10 inches high. Most of the folders looked like official military or VA government type, although somewhat old and dog eared. His silver-rimmed glasses were quite thick, and he had a prominent nose, eyebrows, and a full mustache. He looked like Eugene Levy. One thing about Eugene, he wouldn't shut up. After about five minutes of listening to him gripe about how the military had screwed him over and caused him to lose benefits and rendered him physically disabled, I had to get up and walk around. I surveyed the armory and noticed that the hallways and offices looked like every other military building I'd ever been in—grey, lifeless, dimly lit, yet somehow oddly comforting. I was gone maybe five minutes or so, and then I returned to the briefing room and sat down. Eugene was still talking. He was asking questions of the CSMR recruiters that were, in my opinion, inappropriate for a person who was trying to join such an organization. Finally, the officer in charge of the orientation strode in, introduced himself, and began speaking and showing us a PowerPoint presentation.

The officer in charge was Major Lolly. He was maybe in his early 60s, tall and lanky, and reminded me of one of our commandants at the US Army prison I worked at in Mannheim, West Germany. Sergeant Schultz (I kid you not) accompanied Major Lolly and added an occasional wisecrack or two. My favorite was concerning pay.

"If you're here for the money, you might as well leave. We get nothing, zero...so if it's money you're after, we don't want you," said Sergeant Schultz. Some of the people at the orientation groaned as if this came as a surprise. This news prompted Eugene to interrupt with a loud gasp. He followed this with a scolding tirade aimed at Major Lolly, the essence of which described his sense of disgust that he wouldn't be compensated for his time. He even went as far as to ask for money for attending the orientation.

"But if you enjoy wearing the uniform and continuing to serve, this is the place for you," the major quickly added, cutting off Eugene. Sergeant Schultz took over the presentation covering the history and mission of the CSMR.

The California State Military Reserve (CSMR) is the state defense force of California. The CSMR assists the California

108

National Guard (CNG) in its Homeland Defense mission. The CSMR is under the leadership of the governor of California and cannot be deployed outside of the state. CSMR soldiers aren't paid, and it's strictly a volunteer force. Some CSMR members have prior military service, and some have never even been in the Boy Scouts.

If the CSMR gets deployed within the State of California, then soldiers get paid based on rank. I looked up the California Code governing the CSMR and found out that the governor can deploy them outside of the state if requested by another state (I can only imagine how bad the situation would be to deploy such true weekend warriors outside of the state). The bottom line was that CSMR soldiers are volunteers and don't have to do anything if they don't want to, you can quit at any time, and they can throw you out at any time. The scary part was that when you get called into active duty, you are subject to the Uniform Code of Military Justice (UCMJ).

I was accepted provisionally by the California Center for Military History, Southern Region, in November 2008. Our commander Major Goodluck was a former army aviator and Vietnam veteran. I attended my first drill on November 1, 2008, but I wasn't officially part of the CSMR until December 16, 2008. I had trouble finding our drill location on the Joint Forces Military Training Base at Los Alamitos, California, I couldn't find the building and nobody on the base knew Major Goodluck or anything about the California Center for Military History. I drove around for 30 minutes without success. I called Major Goodluck, but he wasn't answering. Finally, I saw a ramshackle warehouse with the correct building number, building 206. Could that really be our meeting place? It was barely standing, the other buildings around it were condemned and gutted, and huge open pits surrounded the warehouse. I wandered over to the open door by the large warehouse bay door and peeked in sheepishly. There they were. Twelve soldiers in ACUs sat around a few long government grey tables. The warehouse was lit by a few bare light bulbs, and the dusty old building was filled with boxes and other odds and ends of military equipment. A large smiling picture of Governor Arnold Schwarzenegger giving the thumbs-up sign was hanging askew on the wall.

I had served for six years in the active army and a year or so in the army reserves. But this organization was something completely different. Except for a 30-year-old second lieutenant, I was the youngest (at 50) soldier in my unit in the CSMR or SMR as they called it. One man that I sat next to (I'll call him Jim) was even using a walker—he had just had a hip replaced.

"Almost all of us have had to get new body parts," said Jim. All of them were friendly, for sure, but I sensed that this was a very different world than what I had known on active duty. Suddenly I was hit by a startling realization: Holy hell, I think I'm in the militia. I thought of those crazy nuts that Michael Moore filmed in Michigan for his *Bowling for Columbine* film. I then remembered what my friend and fellow teacher, Steve, told me.

"The SMR soldiers are known as Smurfs. I heard that one guy, who hadn't even been in the military, promoted himself to general," he said. Not exactly a comforting thought. Too late, I had already entered the Kingdom of the SMuRfs, and there was no turning back.

We had our first annual training (AT) at Camp San Luis Obispo, California (Camp SLO), in March 2010. I put on my ACUs and started my drive to the camp at 0330 and arrived at 0700. The camp lay just beneath some low-lying coastal mountains that poked up from lush green meadows—it was quite beautiful in the light of the rising sun. My orders were to report

110

to building 719 for registration and administrative instructions. I passed through the gate with a requisite salute from the sergeant and set out to look for building 719. Of course, I couldn't find the building and searched the entire camp until finally, having passed this bland white-washed building without a number many times, I decided to get out and take a closer look. Sure enough, I could see a faint number 719 under a thin coat of white paint on the west wall. There were a few cars parked there, so I parked beneath an old walnut tree and headed into the old building.

Inside building 719, I found Major Goodluck and a female warrant officer who worked at Camp SLO full time. I signed in, and Major Goodluck told me to go and check out the mess hall.

"It's brand new, delicious food, you'll love it!" he said. I had half an hour, so I walked over to the mess hall building. As I walked, I was hit by a wave of nostalgic feelings about being on an army post and eating in army mess halls—essentially, transported back in time. I noticed a lot of young men and women in odd uniforms marching and singing cadences. They seemed to be para-military recruits. I saw more of them at the mess hall in line. After paying six dollars for my breakfast, I got some eggs and sausage and toast and found a few of the CSMR soldiers I knew seated at the far end of a brightly lit mess hall.

"Pretty nice chow hall, huh? And the food is great," said one of my comrades. I nodded in agreement just before I took a bite of my sausage and winced. Oh my god, the mess hall looks nice, but the food is the same as it was in the military prison in Mannheim, West Germany. It might have indeed been the same food as far as I could tell. I discretely brought my napkin to my mouth to unload the unwholesome morsel when the group began to get up and leave. I washed out the terrible flavor from my mouth with watered down orange juice and took a bite of dry wheat toast. That was enough. So much for the new chow hall, and so much for trusting any more of my nostalgic feelings.

The morning started with a briefing by our battalion commander. Colonel French looked, French. He had a thin pencil mustache and had an odd way of holding his chin up very high while he spoke. It seemed rather comical and condescending at the same time. He welcomed us and had us introduce ourselves. There were about 60 people in the room. Once again, other than the young lieutenant from our unit, I was the youngest. But where was the young lieutenant (I called him LT)? I asked Major Goodluck, but he didn't know. The colonel continued, and then someone started knocking on the door by the stage where Colonel French stood. He ignored the knocking at first, but the knocker was persistent, and the sound grew louder. Finally, Colonel French stopped and walked over to open the door and revealed the identity of the insistent knocker. It was our intrepid young lieutenant. I looked over at Major Goodluck and he just rolled his eyes. The LT scurried across the front of the stage and sat down next to me. The LT was apparently unaware that the front door was wide open. The colonel continued. The group consisted of all regions of the California Center for Military History. I recognized the commander of the Naval Historical Unit from the Military Channel and the Discovery Channel, where he served as a show host. He looked like a typical Hollywood, show-biz type because he had a facelift, perfect teeth, and immaculately quaffed grey hair (much longer than military regulations allowed) and groomed to a fare thee well (as my friend and Vietnam War veteran author David Willson would say).

Colonel French told us that the most pressing mission for our Center for Military History was to document and record the unit histories of returning National Guard and Reserve units from California. Operation Iraqi Freedom, Operation Enduring Freedom (OIF/OEF) histories must be preserved, he said. The

112

units are required by Army Field Manual (FM) 1-20 to appoint a unit historical officer, but most don't have the time or the personnel available. It was our job to help preserve unit and individual histories of the Global War on Terror (GWOT). I looked at my fellow chief warrant officer, Chief Lex (who was a CW3), and whispered.

"Our whole mission has changed. I guess the book we were supposed to be writing about Los Alamitos is now on hold?" I said. He agreed. By the way, Chief Lex was an interesting guy. He was a former Special Forces Green Beret who had served in Vietnam. Chief Lex was highly intelligent and had a good sense of humor. He carried a green camouflage rucksack that seemed to contain everything anybody needed magically.

After our morning classes ended, it was time to dig down deep for courage and saunter over to lunch at the mess hall. This time I got a cheeseburger that I figured was a safe bet. I was wrong. But I was lucky compared to one of our female sergeants who got fried chicken, feathers and all. One highlight from lunch was the executive officer, Lieutenant Colonel Shecky. He was hilarious. We returned for afternoon sessions, my stomach heaving from the wretched mess hall food.

In the afternoon, each of the regional commanders, including our commander, gave their reports. We then fell out to the parking lot to have an in-ranks inspection. It felt strange to be in formation, standing at attention, and I slipped back in time again. I had found out during lunch that the young uniformed cadets were part of Camp Grizzly, a special program for at-risk youth. The program used strict military discipline to try to rehabilitate young people in the juvenile court system. It seemed effective from what I could see. As we stood in formation, I noticed a group of Camp Grizzly cadets in formation. In comparison, they made us look old, sick, incompetent, and tired.

Of course, that was because we were old, sick, incompetent, and tired. The Sergeant Major gave us facing movement commands, and half of us responded correctly, and the other half turned the opposite direction or did nothing at all because they couldn't hear the commands. Jarring me back to present reality, I was reminded of why they don't send older folks to war. I passed inspection, although my beret looked like a black mushroom. After the embarrassing inspection in ranks, we moved back inside, thank God, and had a lecture on oral history techniques. I enjoyed the discussion, and we got to see some of an oral history describing a World War II veteran who had flown B-29 bombers and was shot down over Japan. He described his treatment in detail, and it was utterly fascinating. We concluded the day by breaking into non-commissioned officer (NCO) and officer groups and discussed administrative issues. I was glad to leave the camp after that and to head back to Pismo Beach, where I would meet my sweet Ginger that evening.

The average age in the history section of the CSMR was probably 58. Now, I'm not saying that we were too old, but during AT, several people back in Los Angeles called in and reported that the former CSMR commander, General Stevens, had died. This came as a terrible surprise to General Steven's wife, and to General Stevens himself since he was with us at the AT and took the cell phone call from his distraught wife while he was speaking to the troops. He assured her that he was, indeed, very much alive and that the reports of his death were, as Mark Twain once said, "highly exaggerated."

Not wanting to take the risk of eating at the camp mess hall again, I was getting my complimentary breakfast at the Oxford Suites Hotel in Pismo Beach when a tall, middle-aged man approached me. Ginger and I were staying in Pismo Beach during my annual training for the California State Military

Reserve. I was in my ACU uniform and had just been handed my scrambled eggs, bacon, and hash browns.

"Sorry to interrupt your breakfast, but I just wanted to shake your hand and thank you for your service to our country," the man said. My first thought was to tell him that I was only in the CSMR and not a real active-duty soldier. But then I thought that this honesty was probably only for me, not for him. His thanks were heartfelt based on what he thought of all my active duty brothers in sisters in uniform. So, I decided to accept his thanks without any explanation and on behalf of those soldiers, marines, airmen, and sailors who put their lives on the line every day. I smiled shyly and thanked him and wished him a pleasant good morning. Then I went to sit down by myself at a small table by the TV. Ginger was still in bed.

Later that morning, we met at Camp SLO and then got organized into carpools to head to Camp Roberts which was about 40 miles north on Highway 101. I wasn't quick enough to arrange a ride, so by the time I asked around, everyone had a group except for our young lieutenant and Staff Sergeant Teagarden. I asked if they would like me to drive, and they both said yes. There was a reason why no one wanted to ride with these two people. As far as I could tell, they were both savants of some sort–highly intelligent but socially inept. The LT had a dazed look about him and a lazy eye that gave one the impression that he was about to go to sleep. Staff Sergeant Teagarden was a chatterbox know-it-all. He was very tall and overweight and had a head that made you wonder if someone had been playing with the horizontal hold. We started on our drive, and Sergeant Chatterbox didn't stop talking for the entire 45-minute drive.

Staff Sergeant Teagarden had an odd verbal habit of ending every sentence with the phrase, "and such." The two of them carried on unrelated and largely superfluous conversations the whole time. I barely survived. I did find out that LT had been kicked out of this last CSMR unit but didn't explain why. I figured you had to be really annoying to be kicked out of an unpaid, all-volunteer unit. Staff Sergeant Teagarden told me that he was kicked out of the active army while still in basic training, "and such." Both had been in the CSMR for a few years. We finally arrived at Camp Roberts, and I noticed how run down the buildings were, especially compared to Camp SLO. Camp Roberts had over 35,000 soldiers during World War II as it was a major training center. We all met at the Camp Museum and toured through the well laid out, but crowded displays. The museum staff was playing old Bob Hope USO radio shows. We looked at the museum annex, where they had tanks as well. I've always been impressed with tanks, although I know that tankers were often called "spam in a can." We then got back in our vehicles and toured the maneuver area training equipment site (MATES) at the East Garrison of Camp Roberts. That was where the California National Guard stored their equipment for training and mobilization, so they don't have to store it where they drill. This type of storage system saved a lot of wear and tear on the equipment and gave them a centralized maintenance and logistical point.

After the MATES tour, we returned to the main garrison, and I dropped off Staff Sergeant Teagarden. The LT wanted a ride back to Camp SLO but asked if it was okay to take a look at the old World War II barracks. I agreed, reluctantly, and we drove out by the parade field on the north side of the camp facing the freeway. Supposedly, the parade field at Camp Roberts was the largest in the world (the length of 14 football fields). The old barracks buildings seemed to go on for miles, row after row of dilapidated white wooden buildings—450 of them. They were set up in company and battalion groupings with a mess hall, supply room, and headquarters building for each set of barracks. Already

116

transported back in time again, I began to get a haunting feeling as we drove by these buildings realizing that they held nearly 35,000 troops during the height of training for World War II. We got out of the car and began walking around the decaying structures. A wind was blowing, but all else was silent as if frozen in time. I felt the presence of all those soldiers that had passed through the camp. Some of whom never returned home from war. I heard their voices echoing and the sound of their boots on the gravel road and a distant bugle call. It was a military ghost town.

We spotted the old chapel at the end of one of the rows of barracks. The chapel was in equally bad shape. The wind was blowing through the broken windowpanes making an eerie whistling noise. It was frightening, sad, and nostalgic all at the same time. I could see the ghosts of the soldiers and the noise of jeeps and the bustling training camp as it was in 1943. Big band music seemed to be playing in some far-off place. Some of the buildings were almost totally collapsed, others stood brave and tall against the relentless elements although extremely weathered. Mother Nature was taking back what man had created. In this post-apocalyptic setting, bushes, grass, and trees were overtaking the falling structures.

Returning to the present day as I left the camp with the old barracks rows in my rear-view mirror, I couldn't help but think that we are also like these buildings. We serve our purpose in our youth and prime of life, then we grow old, useless, fall apart, and are abandoned until we ultimately disintegrate into dust and are forgotten.

In retrospect, my time in the military wasn't a failure. I simply failed to understand its significance and how I continued after my discharge to serve in other ways. I honored my veteran comrades through my teaching about war, bringing a broader understanding to young students who likely and hopefully won't

117

ever have to learn firsthand. I guess my job, and my mission, as a historian in a world that suffers from historical amnesia, was to help people understand the true nature of war, and honor the dignity of our forbearers and preserve their memories if nothing else. My sense of mission led to my founding the Citrus College veterans program and, with the help of Ginger and my friend Manny, put together the first transition college course for returning veterans in our nation's history—Boots to Books. I have come to realize that I didn't need to be in uniform again to heal from the past. I was in a different position now, a different role that didn't require me to be a soldier. I had evolved and so had my mission. It was now clear. I felt this transformation as I walked like a ghost through the ruins of Camp Roberts' abandoned barracks. Ultimately, by reaching into the past for answers, I discovered that the change, the fix, and the healing I needed was internal, not external. I resigned from the CSMR on September 10, 2010. Although we should always remember the past and learn from it, we can't live in the past; we must move on, just as future generations will do when they leave us behind and build on what we have achieved.

Sajajid (2010)

"What is the spirit of the bayonet!" shouted the drill sergeant as he paced menacingly back and forth in front of the raw recruits.

"To kill, to kill, to kill, drill sergeant!" screamed the recruits in unison. The preceding exchange represents a typical experience for those soldiers, like myself, who were going through basic training and left a deep impression on me to this day 40 years later. The military is very good at taking away your fear of killing. No matter what your job in the military, the death of another human being is a possible outcome of your actions. Carl Jung wrote about the duality of man—all of us are part warrior and part peacemaker. Our hard-wired instincts allow us to kill. It's part of our fight or flight mechanism housed in the brain stem—our reptilian brain. The military doesn't create warriors; they bring the warrior out that is already inside of all of us. I know that sounds a bit like Mr. Miyagi in *Karate Kid*, but it's true. Then, the military trains the warrior with the requisite skills he or she will need for war. To be able to kill, you must desensitize yourself to the act of killing. You must dehumanize the enemy. Sometimes warriors get caught up in the madness of war. I've heard stories and seen photos of severed ears, tongues, genitals, and other body parts. You no longer fear the dark when you become one with the darkness.

Many of my students, veterans, and non-veterans have become friends of mine. I invited Peck, a former student, to come back to the class and speak about his nightmarish experiences as a marine. He told us that during the battle of Hue in 1968, he saw a pile of rotting human corpses. The stench was unbearable. He noticed a large pig feasting on the human remains. Someone in his platoon shot the pig because he couldn't take it anymore. Peck

119

said that the act of killing in the war did not seem real to him until he went home to Seattle on leave. During an acid party in the University District, where he was the only veteran, a few long-haired guys came up to him and asked him if he was aware of what he was doing over there in Vietnam. Up to that point, Peck hadn't paid much attention. It was as if he was on a hunting trip, he said. Peck didn't return to Vietnam.

Nurses in Vietnam suffered more than people think. Combat soldiers saw more than their share of blood and guts when they fought, but nurses and doctors saw much more. They saw the flower of youth reduced to legless, armless, and faceless patients often without futures or dreams. Lara, my nurse friend, told me about her struggles with PTSD. As part of her duties as a surgical nurse in Vietnam, Lara would wash surgical sponges in a series of water and soap solutions contained in metal drums. The surgical sponges contained bits of skin, other tissue, and blood clots. Sometimes these things would rise to the surface of the water in the drums. She began to experience nightmares after her return to the States, nightmares where the faces of dead soldiers she had treated appeared in each of the drums of water.

Another friend of mine, Max, was in three wars—World War II, Korea, and Vietnam. I called him "The Eternal Warrior." His happy-go-lucky attitude was infectious for my young students. Max would tell us about the 12-year old girl that he shot near the village of Buon Ma Thuot in the Central Highlands of South Vietnam. He still had nightmares decades after the shooting. Max was not, however, bothered by others whom he had to kill in war. As he said, he felt that he was merely doing his job.

Max once went to the hospital in Seattle to visit a man who had been shot randomly by a freeway sniper. The shooting had left him paralyzed and in a wheelchair. Max met with him, and the man said that he didn't want pity. Max told the man that he was mistaken. Max wanted help from him. Max told the man about how he had shot the 12-year old girl in Vietnam. He told him how sorry he was. Max wanted forgiveness. The man in the wheelchair was happy that he could help someone else and not focus on his despair. Max even wrote a letter to the government of Vietnam in 1995 and explained what happened over 30 years ago in that little village. He never received a reply.

My friend, I'll call him Melvin, served in Iraq. Like many warriors, he took home some souvenirs from his time in that deadly war zone. He collected the prayer rugs (*sajajid* in Arabic) belonging to each of the people he killed. Melvin stores them in a box in his garage. They're all bloodstained, and he says that they haunt him. He can't bear to look at them *or* throw them away. I offered to dispose of the prayer rugs for him. After I made that offer, I began to worry. I wondered what I would do with them. Would I burn them? Would I throw them away? Then I came up with the idea of giving the rugs to a local mosque for the imam to handle in some honorable and dignified way. This dilemma, in some ways, reminded me that over the 24 years that I've taught the Vietnam War history course, dozens of people had given me personal effects from their loved ones who served and died in Vietnam or as a result of their service. My office at Citrus College was filled with these haunting items.

Every day that I sat at my office desk and tried to concentrate and do some work or counsel the occasional students who took advantage of my office hours, I stared at these pieces of shattered lives and physical reminders of grief from over fifty years ago. I recently decided that I couldn't carry this burden any longer. I boxed up all the items, including the bronze star medal that my friend Carl had earned. Carl committed suicide in 2002 after suffering for decades with severe PTSD. His picture stared back at me as I graded papers and seemed to ask for some resolution, understanding, and some sense of closure. I couldn't take it anymore, so I gave Carl's photo, bronze star, and all the other items to my friend Steve who runs a military museum. At the museum, researchers will be able to study the items and preserve history. They will likely not have the personal connection that I had. I went further and decided to stop teaching the Vietnam course. I handed it over to Steve. The course was taking a toll on me, and I couldn't watch the films, discuss the tragedy, and see the pain on the faces of my young students contemplating that war any longer. Especially difficult was seeing my young veteran students learning about their war by studying the Vietnam War and suddenly realize what had happened to them—used up and abandoned, just as it happened to previous generations of American servicemen and women. I had put in more than two decades of service in protecting the Vietnam War story from political manipulation. I was tired and worn down.

I still serve the veterans at my college in a more indirect way, staying in the shadows, and helping where and when I can. A former student veteran asked me why I tell them to get help from the Veterans Administration (VA) but have not sought help myself. I'm still impacted by my time in the service, and I'm now officially a disabled veteran. I still hear the echoes of the bayonet chant in my dreams. Luckily, I suppose, my troubled warrior friend Melvin never gave me the prayer rugs, so I imagine they're still in a box, in the dark recesses of his garage, out of sight, but not out of mind. Their existence quietly reminds Melvin every day of the madness and cruelty of war, and of the darkness that he must carry with him for the rest of his life.

It Hasta be Shasta (2015)

When I was a kid growing up in Seattle, I remember Shasta brand soda pop. The image of Mt. Shasta was on each can. It was a popular brand because it was cheaper than Coca Cola, Pepsi, Sprite, and 7-up and because Shasta offered many different flavors, including chocolate soda. Almost every kids' birthday party I went to had Shasta soda pop and Kool-Aid. By the way, I never drank soda pop until I was 17 years old because it hurt my throat. I know, I'm weird. I knew Mt. Shasta was in California, but I had only seen Mt. Rainier and Mt. St. Helens and Mt. Adams, all in Washington State. It wasn't until I was 11 years old that I traveled to California with my parents to see the coastal redwoods in 1969. At the Trees of Mystery roadside attraction in Klamath, California, we saw a marvelous sight, and I don't mean the redwoods, although they were cool, I'm talking about the 49-foot-tall Paul Bunyan and his 35-foot-tall friend, Babe the Blue Ox. Paul would move his head, wink, and wave as he greeted visitors. I remember him making my mom laugh when he called her out. "Hey, pretty blonde lady, where you from?" I was totally impressed.

Since my childhood, I have traveled from Washington to California and back many times and have always marveled at Mt. Shasta. At first sight, I noticed that it gave off a mysterious aura and that has stuck with me ever since. In 2015, my wife Ginger and I decided to drive to Seattle in a rather circuitous route. The occasion was to retrieve some family items from my sister's estate after she passed away suddenly in December 2014. We set out from our home in Glendora, California, to Las Vegas taking the 210 freeway west to the 15 freeway north. After passing through Las Vegas, we took Highway 93 through eastern Nevada. Highway 93 is known as one of the most desolate stretches of highway in America. For hour-long stretches of time, we drove alone and passed no other vehicles.

As we drove through Nevada at one point, we were only 50 miles to the east of Area 51 and Groom Lake. Area 51 is a highly classified remote detachment of Edwards Air Force Base, and the airspace around it is restricted. The government didn't formally acknowledge its existence until 2013. Some say that it's just a testing site for the development of experimental aircraft and weapons systems, while others say that Area 51 is one of the central components of the secret space program surrounding the UFO phenomena. Bob Lazar's *Dreamland* is a good book on the subject.

A former student of mine who was assigned as part of the US Air Force security forces at Groom Lake told me that he saw UFOs and other strange things at the facility. One night, he and his partner stumbled on something unusual out in the desert. They heard voices and laughing. When they hit their bright white spotlights, there was nothing, but when they used their infrared scopes, they saw people. The people, or whatever they were, then vanished. On another night, they saw fast-moving objects in the sky making no noise that were not part of the American military inventory. All of this added to the mystique of desolation as we drove.

This spring break getaway of 2015 was truly a desolation trip. For some unknown reason, I felt compelled to navigate through eastern Nevada. It was like I was compelled to do so. One of our stops was the Great Basin National Park. This national park is one of the least known and least visited national parks. Just one summer before our visit, a park ranger found an 1860 Henry Golden Boy rifle that had been leaning against a tree since the late 1800s. Now that is a sign of how remote that place was. Great Basin National Park is the home of the oldest trees on Earth—the bristlecone pine. These trees have a twisted shape and survive at high altitudes. Each root of the bristlecone supports only one part of the tree so that one section of the tree can die, but other parts keep on living. We drove as high up as we could go to hit the snowline. It was fun to wander around and have an impromptu snowball fight. No one was around, we were alone, and so it was a bit spooky as nightfall was fast approaching. I felt the spirits of early mountain men and Indians. It was time to leave.

After eating dinner at the Cellblock Steakhouse and spending the night in the Jailhouse Hotel in Ely, Nevada, we drove to Idaho and eventually into Oregon's Blue Mountains, where we stopped at a hotel in Baker City. As we drove through the Blue Mountains, it started to snow, big heavy wet snowflakes. We eventually made our way to Washington State through the tri-cities, home of the Hanford Reservation, where they produced plutonium for atomic bombs. After crossing through Yakima, we approached Snoqualmie Pass as the skies were growing dark and we got caught in a spring blizzard. It was touch and go for over an hour with nearly zero visibility. We had no chains. Luckily, the blizzard let up on the western side of the Cascade Mountains.

We took care of preserving some family heirlooms and headed back South to California using the more conventional well-traveled route on Interstate 5. It was getting late when we crossed Siskiyou Pass and into California. Passing through Yreka, we spotted Mt. Shasta. Ginger suggested we take some scenic routes. I felt apprehensive, but we did it anyway. It was dusk as we drove around Mt. Shasta on Highways 97, 18, 13, and then 89. I was so nervous, unexplainably so. The mountain had a mysterious aura and was so enormous and imposing. I felt frightened by the mountain, and I felt like something was going to happen. It was desolate and there were no other cars. Finally, we did see something. A car was pulled over to the side of the road that had hit a deer. Ginger suggested that we should stop and see if they needed assistance. I didn't stop, and the people just stared at us as we drove by. I thought they looked strange, almost unnatural. My gut was telling me not to trust them. I wouldn't stop, which annoyed Ginger, but I felt a need to keep going as quickly as possible.

Mt. Shasta is considered by many people to be one of the most sacred places on Earth and is often called the magical mountain. The mountain is over 14,000 feet high and very broad. There are many legends about the mountain, originating with the Native Americans who considered the area to be sacred. The Native people, such as the Shasta, Modoc, Wintun, Atsugewi, and Klamath tribes, had been living around the mountain for more than 9,000 years. They considered Mt. Shasta to be the center of creation. They still perform rituals to honor the mountain and attract the spiritual power that it emanates.

Some people believe that Mt. Shasta is home to secret alien underground bases, and there have been numerous UFO sightings in the area and some disappearances. Local people have reported tall humanoids in the small towns around the mountain. Others believe that a reptilian race of aliens lives inside of the mountain and use it as an energy supply base. Frederick S. Oliver wrote a book entitled *A Dweller on Two Planets* in 1884 that details how the mountain has underground tunnels where descendants of the Atlanteans live. In 1971, Buddhists built a monastery by Mt. Shasta. They believe it is a focal point of positive energy. Legend has it that a wildfire in 1931 was put out by a mysterious fog emanating from the mountain.

I can't verify or deny any of these stories, all that I can say is that the area around the mountain made me very nervous and I'm almost certain that those motorists who had hit a deer were up to no good. Maybe they were aliens disguised as motorists, and it was another attempt to abduct me? I'm simply not sure.

Thinking in Time (2017)

"History...is a nightmare from which I am trying to awake."

–James Joyce, *Ulysses*

"As we know, reality is not a function of the event as event, but of the relationship of that event to past, and future, events. We seem to here have a paradox: that the reality of event, which is not real in itself, arises from other events which, likewise, in themselves are not real. But this only affirms what we must affirm: that direction is all. And only as we realize this do we live, for our own identity is dependent on this principle."

–Robert Penn Warren, *All the King's Men*

British historian E.H. Carr wrote that history is "an unending dialogue between the past and present." We are influenced by the present when we write about the past, and we are influenced by the past when writing about today. However insightful, it all sounds rather fluid and not very useful. How can we make use of history then? *Thinking in Time: The Uses of History for Decision Makers*, was a book by Richard E. Neustadt and Ernest R. May, published in 1988. The two academics used historical case studies to develop lessons on how to improve decision-making in government. History is useful, but it seems to me that historians are no longer being asked to help those in power in Washington, DC. Instead, politicians rely on political operatives who tend to have a weak grasp on history and often seek quick, short-term solutions to challenging problems. However, this lack of historical perspective isn't unique to our elected government officials, as we're all suffering from a national case of historical amnesia.

Although I generally agree with Neustadt and May, my definition of thinking in time is much more personal. I believe in making history useful, but I also believe that history begins and ends with the individual. We don't have to wait for our national leaders to learn the lessons from the past, we can learn and apply those lessons ourselves. From my historian's perspective, I believe we can identify useful patterns and cycles in history and apply them to help us today as we prepare for the future.

Like most people, I'm not just one thing, and I wear many hats. I weave my paranormal experiences into the classroom and my historical works. If we introduce the paranormal into this discussion of thinking in time, it gets even more interesting. My spirit friends have told me that in the spirit realm, there is no future and no past. Albert Einstein once said that "Time and space are not conditions of existence, time and space is a model for thinking." He also said: "A human being is a part of the whole called by us universe; a part limited in time and space. He experiences himself, his thoughts, and his feelings as something separate from the rest—a kind of optical delusion of consciousness." Knowing that we can communicate with the dead in the spirit world opens a potentially unlimited source of knowledge for us. For example, I made a connection with the late Senator John McCain. In a series of discussions, he helped me put many current events into perspective and even asked me not to share some of those specifics due to national security. What other historical figures can we contact and ask for advice? Think of all the wisdom the valuable insights we could gain. We've already utilized remote viewing to gather intelligence information independent of time and space. I think this is called psychic archaeology.

The Stargate Project successfully employed remote viewers who provided valuable information about enemy capabilities and projects and the location of missing government officials. I spoke to Lyn Buchanan, who was one of the military remote viewers, and he told me that he is still answering his nation's call to service. In his book *The Seventh Sense*, Lyn wrote: "If you want to improve your soul and spirit and well-being, learn a way to bring home a missing child. There is nothing like it in either the real or ethereal world. CRV (controlled remote viewing) deepens your character and forever changes your life for the better. And believe it or not, that is only a mere side effect." Project Stargate ended in 1995, officially, but I strongly suspect and sincerely hope that we are still using remote viewing to enhance our intelligence gathering system. To not do so would certainly be folly.

It's time for a historical exercise along these lines. Let's go back to Tuesday, November 8, 2016, dear readers. I knew that there was a possibility that Donald Trump would win, and discussions with my political science colleagues confirmed that, but still, I went to bed that night certain that Hillary Clinton would be the 45th president of the United States. When I woke up the next day, I discovered that Donald Trump had been elected. I had this odd feeling that something unusual had happened, something out of our control, something paranormal perhaps. It was as if I was in an episode of the *Twilight Zone*. I'm not particularly political and don't belong to either political party so I can speak my mind free from the hindrance of any party loyalty. Honestly, I wasn't a supporter of either candidate. As is so often the case in a two-party system, you end up voting for the one who will do the least harm or the lesser of two evils, as some say. I've concluded that Donald Trump was elected for a reason that is still unclear to most people in the United States and abroad, and maybe even unclear to those who are his most ardent supporters. He serves a transitional role as we enter into a paradigm shift in our political system. This shift occurs approximately every 40 years. A paradigm shift originates with the people and is projected upward through the political parties.

Few could have predicted that a billionaire businessman and reality TV star like Donald Trump would win the Republican nomination, much less the presidency. Hillary Clinton was a more obvious candidate, but Senator Bernie Sanders put up a good fight, and eventually, Clinton prevailed with possibly some assistance from an archaic and corrupt Democratic Party nomination system. It's perhaps an odd comparison, but Trump's rise is somewhat like the rise of Jimmy Carter in the 1976 election. A vote for Jimmy Carter was a vote against the Washington establishment. The Republican convention in Cleveland was a grandiose tribute to Trump's impossible mission as a billionaire populist. His rise confounded the Republican party establishment and splintered it into several pieces. The 2016 Democratic Convention in Philadelphia was more of a neo-liberal coronation of Hillary Clinton with Senator Sanders officially giving his blessing, which irritated his fervent supporters.

Most people on the left and right agree that powerful corporations have influenced politics and both political parties. Are we returning to the Gilded Age of cronyism? What can we make of the 2016 presidential election cycle? We know that more than half of the money pouring into Super Political Action Committees (PACs) comes from just 50 mega-rich donors (both Liberals and Conservatives). The last time wealth factored into politics this directly was in 1896 when corporations and banks helped put Republican William McKinley in the White House. This influence by the super-wealthy was all made possible today because the Supreme Court decided in *Citizens United v. Federal Election Commission* that the government could not restrict

132

independent political expenditures by a nonprofit corporation. Where does that leave the average citizen looking for responsive government representation? We need to look back for an answer.

The original Gilded Age came to an end when both parties supported organized labor, a federal income tax, antitrust enforcement, and financial regulation, as part of what became known as the Progressive Era (1900-1920). Now, Republicans and Democrats have worked together to cement the two-party system and dismantle the remnants of the New Deal social welfare state. Both parties court populist grassroots causes and issues that divide Liberals and Conservatives, but the parties at their core are more alike than different. Today's populism may be false. As distasteful as Donald Trump is to many folks, he has pointed out something very ugly in our political system. People are easily distracted, manipulated, and divided while the wealthiest retain their power and control. Bernie Sanders generated enthusiasm, especially among Millennials. I believe he could have beaten Donald Trump because Sanders represented change, and Clinton didn't.

Critics often compare President Trump to Adolf Hitler. I'm hesitant to use the Hitler analogy because it's so often misused, I mean if everyone you hate is Hitler, who was Hitler? Donald Trump reminds me, sometimes, of Italian fascist dictator Benito Mussolini in his mannerisms, but that characterization isn't quite correct either. I believe he is more like P.T. Barnum, Buffalo Bill Cody, or any of the men responsible for the construction of the transcontinental railroad. All of them were truly iconic American figures, visionary, creative, driven, egotistical, financially successful, and, let's face it, rather shady—the American way.

In a Monmouth University poll in May 2019, 44 percent of Americans said that Russia interfered in our 2016 election, and

29 percent said that they probably interfered. The Russians have done this in other elections around the world. Of course, our CIA does the same thing. I believe their main goal is to spread fear and anger and divide our nation. It's important to keep in mind that the Russians can't defeat America, only we can do that if we allow differences and divisions to tear us apart. America needs to remain strong and united to handle the challenges that lie ahead. Intelligence experts warn that at least 90 nations are either already unstable or will be shortly; we are facing challenging times.

In his novel *1984*, George Orwell wrote: "Those who control the present, control the past and those who control the past control the future." We, the people, must control our destiny. He went on to write that "the most effective way to destroy people is to deny and obliterate their own understanding of their history." We must take ownership of our history and think for ourselves. Orwell warns us that "until they become conscious they will never rebel, and until after they have rebelled they cannot become conscious." A conundrum for sure, but the direction is clear, toward the liberation of the body, mind, soul, and our consciousness. Orwell reminds us that "reality exists in the human mind, and nowhere else."

As useful as history it, we must be careful in using history because we can't impose our thinking and beliefs on those in the past, for they lived under a different set of circumstances and a foundation of existence unique to their time. Was George Washington just an immoral slave-owner? Was Abraham Lincoln a racist? Were Dr. Martin Luther King, Jr., and President John F. Kennedy just misogynistic philanderers and nothing else? Is no one worth looking up to or emulating? Where does it end? Without heroes, our nation will be deconstructed, unforgiven, and irreparable. Many people want to erase history and purge it of all people and things that are, by today's standards, offensive. If that trend continues, all history will be erased, and we'll have nothing to help guide us. We'll be left rudderless to drift at the mercy of the winds of shifting public opinion with no control, uncertain of the future, and blind to the past. Truth is the truth, uncomfortable, or not. As I tell my history students, if you're uncomfortable, you're learning.

Another way to look at the concept of thinking in time is from a musical perspective. When you're in time, you are in sync with the rest of the musicians, and the rhythm of the song. Thinking in time is to be in sync with the world, past, the fleeting present, and the undetermined future, simultaneously. In other words, thinking in time means you are in sync with time itself, standing ready at the tiller, steering a course to your ultimate destiny.

Returning to the James Joyce and Robert Penn Warren quotes at the beginning of this story, how can we awaken from the nightmare and find our moorings? Robert Penn Warren suggests that the reality of an event is based on relationships to other events, past, and future. As my dear departed friend Gene said after his death: "There is no past, there is no future, there is only the eternal now." Reality is what we create moment to moment as the currents of time flow in all directions at once. The direction of the moment is what we have. Expectations are anathema to us because they're presumptuous and often lead to disappointment, frustration, and anger. Once we let go of the unhealthy desires and expectations that cause us such pain and become fully awake and conscious, we experience what in rotorcraft aerodynamics is called translational lift and what surfers experience when they catch a wave. The power of the universe carries you. We go as we flow and do the best we can to love and honor the life we have and those lives around us, as we are all part of the same consciousness and connected to the infinite.

Hawkeye (2018)

I've always loved animals. When I was a little boy, my mom said I could imitate almost any animal. We had cats when I was growing up. They were my friends more so than pets. I loved the stories my dad told about the Kodiak bears in Alaska. My friends and I used to watch the salmon spawn every fall in the stream that ran through our neighborhood. On camping trips with my parents, my brother Alf and I delighted in feeding peanuts to the ground squirrels and witnessing how the blue jays would steal our food from the picnic table and even make passes at hot frying pans over the campfire. I would watch nature shows with my parents, *Mutual of Omaha's Wild Kingdom,* or the *Undersea World of Jacques Cousteau.* Wonderful memories.

We don't have any animals in the house now because my wife Ginger is deathly allergic to fur-bearing creatures. It's sad, especially for her because she also loves animals, and they love her. However, in some ways, it's a blessing that we can't have animals because of how sad it was when my animal friends died. I still grieve the loss of my cat Tiger, a true-blue companion who acted more like a dog than a cat. He met me at the bottom of our long driveway after school when the bus dropped me off. His timing was impeccable. We would play chase all the way up the steep driveway to our home on the hill. Where we live now in Glendora, California, we have a lot of wildlife around our house. Because we're in the foothills of the San Gabriel Mountains, we get bears, bobcats, coyotes, skunks, raccoons, and many other creatures roaming through our yard. We also have a family of red-tailed hawks who live in our neighborhood and hunt for mice, rats, and rabbits in the vacant lot on the hill above our house.

On August 20, 2014, which marked the 15th anniversary of my father's death, I was greeted as I returned from my morning run by a large red-tailed hawk on a lamp post on our street. I stopped to look up at this magnificent bird of prey. He was a big male, as best I could tell, and was perched just above my head and let out his hoarse screaming screech three times like he was trying to tell me something. He looked at me, and I looked at him. We probably stood like this for one minute observing each other. I felt like it was a getting-to-know-each-other meeting. Then, with one long sustained screech, he flew off, flapping his magnificent wings. Looking back, I know that this started a spiritual awakening for me. I had seen the hawks before, but after this meeting, I felt connected to them and their role in the neighborhood. Hawkeye and I became friends.

In the past four years, I have gone through many changes in my life. I had begun to concentrate on those things that are most important and living for those things that matter and bring joy to me, my family, my friends, and others. My older sister Bjørg died in 2014, and my colleague and friend Maia was found dead in her home in Idaho in 2015. After a return of his lung cancer, my dear childhood friend Gene passed away in 2016. As all these losses took place in the past few years, I watched the red-tailed hawk family grow, with young ones being taught to hunt and soar high above our neighborhood under the watchful eyes of their parents. Meeting Hawkeye four years ago began the spiritual transformation that led me to write *Timeless*, my first paranormal book, and teaching a paranormal class at Citrus in the fall of 2018. The message that the red-tailed hawk gave me was one of connection to the spirit world; he served as a messenger from the great beyond. I did some research on hawks and found out how important they are for cultures around the world.

The red-tailed hawk is one of the most common hawks in North America and can be found from Alaska to Panama. They are also known as chicken hawks even though they don't usually prey on chickens. The red-tailed hawk can be seen in a wide range of habitats like deserts, forests, farmland, and urban areas, and are legally protected in Canada, Mexico, and the United States by the Migratory Bird Treaty Act. Red-tailed hawks can also vary significantly in color, from black to white.

Legend has it that when a hawk swoops into your life, you should be ready for a higher level of awareness and an enhancement to the development of your mind and spirit. Indigenous people believed that hawks were messengers from the angels and God. The hawk signals to us a time to focus on what lies ahead and our responsibilities. Our friend, the hawk, encourages us to fly higher than we ever thought we could and guides us in our awakening to the spirit world. Native Americans believe that hawks help us to trust our inner guidance and a higher sense of self as we gain psychic abilities and vision. The hawk teaches us to patiently observe from far above with a keen eye and then take swift, decisive action when necessary. If a red-tailed hawk has soared into your life, you're lucky because you'll be in a position to help others through your newfound perspective, strength, and vision.

I chose the name Hawkeye for the red-tailed hawk that befriended me several years ago for many reasons. The fictional character Hawkeye from James Fenimore Cooper's five *Leatherstocking Tales* books (including *The Last of the Mohicans*) was originally known as Natty Bumppo. Natty was white and grew up with the Delaware Indians. As an adult, he was a fearless warrior skilled in the use of many different types of weapons. He was often accompanied by his Mohican foster brother Chingachgook and nephew Uncas. There is a Marvel comics hero named Hawkeye, who is part of the Avengers team. Hawkeye doesn't have any superhuman powers, but he is in top physical condition and is an expert archer, swordsman, and acrobat. He can turn any object into a weapon. When he first appeared in Marvel comics in 1964, he was a villain who grew up in a carnival and was trained by criminals but became a hero when he joined the Avengers a year later in 1965.

Hawkeye was also a character in the movie and TV series *M*A*S*H*. Alan Alda played army surgeon Benjamin "Hawkeye" Pierce in the TV series. Daniel Day-Lewis portrayed Hawkeye in the 1992 film *The Last of the Mohicans*. Because red-tailed hawks are also known as chicken hawks, it reminded me of the best-selling book *Chickenhawk* by Vietnam War helicopter pilot Robert Mason. I met Robert and his wife Patience when I helped my mentor, Vietnam War author David Willson, put on a Vietnam War Writers Symposium in 1998. I flew Huey helicopters (UH-1), like Robert, but in the peacetime army. We all read his book in flight school.

My friend Hawkeye died on November 14, 2018. I saw him many times in the past four years circling overhead, perched on lampposts and trees, calling out to me, and advising me. He was a trusted friend who watched over my family and me. He was the grandfather of the red-tailed hawks in our neighborhood. Where he once stood, proud, defiant, ever vigilant, determined, majestic, noble, and precise, I saw him on that sad day lying in the street below a giant oak tree. Hawkeye was gone. I rescued him from careless drivers who would run him over and desecrate his body and brought him home. I called the Fish and Wildlife Service, but no one answered the phone. I then called the Inland Valley Humane Society, and they said they would come out the next day and retrieve Hawkeye. Later, I learned that my Norwegian friend Åge's beautiful strawberry blonde middle daughter committed suicide in a forest north of Oslo at about the same time that Hawkeye died. I broke down and cried in my VA therapist's office the next day talking about Hawkeye and thinking about my friend's daughter. The sadness was overwhelming. But then, I thought, Hawkeye would want me to carry on and continue to fly the mission, soaring into the spirit world to provide the bridge for our loved ones here in the physical world, remaining ever vigilant, serving valiantly without fear, and with great purpose and honor. Thank you, Hawkeye my friend, we'll meet again.

Take Me to Your Leader (2018)

"The world's most powerful individuals are actually shape-shifting reptilians." I was a bit taken aback when I heard these words in the introduction to the *Beyond Reality* radio show as I was preparing for my first interview with Jason Hawes (of the old TV show *Ghost Hunters* and a new one, *Ghost Nation*) and J.V. Johnson publisher of *TAPS ParaMagazine*. I shared the evening with Terry Lovelace, the former Assistant Attorney General for American Somoa, and US Air Force veteran. Terry had been abducted by aliens a few times and had also been implanted. My first few radio interviews were strictly about telepathy, clairvoyance, ghosts, hauntings and demons. The basic paranormal stuff detailed in my first *Timeless* book. Little did I know that on August 6, 2018, I was to get my personal introduction to the world of outworlders and abduction.

After our radio interview, Terry and I became friends. I read his book, *Incident at Devil's Den*, and then I asked Terry to be the second guest on my *Timeless Esoterica* radio show. As I became more familiar with his story, I grew slightly more paranoid. The full realization was setting in. Have my suspicions about aliens been confirmed? Were there aliens among us? Had I been abducted? Certainly, I had had many strange paranormal experiences in my life, but were any of them related to aliens? I researched information on alien abduction, and the most frequently reported indicators or effects of alien abduction are:

1. lost time,

2. unexplained markings on the body,

3. hearing humming noises at night,

4. the feeling of being watched, especially at night,

5. low self-esteem,

6. strange medical conditions,

7. fear of closets, cupboards,

8. obsessive-compulsive tendencies,

9. hyper-vigilance,

10. a strange electronic device is implanted,

11. feeling special or chosen, and a

12. sense of levitation or flying.

I have felt or have exhibited all but one of these things. I don't think that I have an implant, but then again, I've only had limited X-rays, so who knows. I stumbled across some information on blood types, and the negative blood type anomaly and connection to aliens. I wrote about this in my story "Anzar's Answers" in *Timeless Deja Vu*. My research and interest have continued as I have sought to discover the connection between the paranormal, ghosts, spirits, and aliens. Not long after my interview on *Beyond Reality*, I was offered my own radio show. I named the show *Timeless Esoterica*. My first guest was Dr. Dean Radin, the chief scientist at the Institute of Noetic Sciences (IONS). Dr. Radin had been involved with the Star Gate Project, a top-secret US government psychic spy project from 1971 to 1995. Has our government has been lying to us about aliens all along? Or, worse yet, have they been collaborating with them? Once you start down a path like this one, it is hard to turn back.

A remarkable thing happened after months of trying to contact them, the executive producer for George Noory's *Coast to Coast AM* radio show called and wanted to interview me. My book and my story got out to millions of listeners on October 29, 2018, and book sales soared. They say everything comes with a price. My national radio show appearance was no exception. The very next day, I received emails and phone calls. Some people were very nice and others were, let's just say, a bit off-kilter. One person who contacted me was a retired scientist who had run a psychic research lab at Stanford University in the 1970s and 80s. Dr. Edwin M. Young told me that the space program was a cover-up for what was really going on and that there was a secret space program. He recommended many different government whistleblowers for me to check out. Having read a lot about quantum physics and its relationship to the paranormal, I sent him my theoretical model, what I call my personal quantum reality. Dr. Young told me that it's quite simple, as I wrote in the prologue to this book, matter constantly vibrates in and out of our reality and is a condensed form of energy that is guided by mind focus and powered by spirit. I believe that the aliens know this and we, the great majority of us, are kept in the dark.

Dr. Young commented on my personal quantum reality model that I published in *Timeless Deja Vu*.

"Your model makes a good attempt at removing the illusion of time from an entity's flow of experiences…For me, the value of the particle-wave concept (developed from certain perplexing experimental issues) is actually related to the "fact" (in my world) that matter vibrates in and out of this material construct—which is not yet recognized (actually, not allowed to be recognized, but now we're into conspiracies) in conventional science." I hold a regular correspondence with Dr. Young and bounce ideas and concepts off him all the time.

Startling realizations are unnerving. It's not that I hadn't thought about aliens existing or visiting us, it's just that now I had some validation of these thoughts and experiences. I began to ask my spirit guides about any possible alien contact that I might have had (at that point, I only suspected that I had been

145

contacted). In September, I asked my spirit friends Gene and Maia about aliens.

"To survive, that is why they are here," said both Gene and Maia.

"We are the aliens," added Gene. I wrote about this concept of alien lineage in *Timeless Deja Vu*. I recently read a book, *Identified Flying Objects*, by Dr. Michael Masters, a professor at Montana Tech, in Butte, Montana. He contends that the UFOs and alien contacts are actually our descendants from the distant future. In other words, time-traveling humans, not aliens. It's an intriguing theory.

I decided to consult an unusual government source. I had made contact with Senator John McCain after his death, and he has told me some interesting things. In October 2018, I had a spiritual conversation with the senator.

"We have contacted aliens, they are helping us with telepathy, some are good, some are bad," he said. My brother-in-law Carl Orlob knew John McCain while they were in the navy and training in Pensacola. Senator McCain was a naval aviator and was shot down over North Vietnam and held and tortured for nearly six years in the infamous Hanoi Hilton. I didn't agree with every position Senator McCain took, but I sure respected him. I should say that in this life, Senator McCain was the only Washington politician who personally answered my letters. And he wasn't even my senator. I think that says something about him. A few weeks later, probably with aliens on my mind, I had some terribly frightening images pop into my head while I woke up in the darkness one night. I saw vivid images of reptilian aliens. Was it a repressed memory? As it turned out, yes, it was (see my story "Special Processing" in this book).

Just before Halloween 2018, I connected with Phil Schneider, a UFO Secret Space Program whistleblower. Phil was an ex-government engineer who claimed to have been involved with building top-secret underground bases. He also claimed that he was one of only three people to survive a firefight between large grey aliens and US military forces at the Dulce underground base in New Mexico. In January 1996, he was beaten and murdered in his apartment. Through my walking meditation, I was able to reach him in the spirit world.

"Phil, were you murdered? And by whom?" I asked.

"Yes...government and the aliens," he said. He was very matter of fact and didn't hesitate in answering.

"My dreams of reptilian aliens, what can you tell me?" I asked.

"They are on to you." My fear was building.

"What do they want?" I asked, almost not wanting to know the answer.

"DNA, and your connection to the original progenitor," he said. Oh great, another big worry.

"What can I do?" I asked.

"It's out of the box, can't put the genie back in the bottle, stay in the limelight, don't be alone. I wanted the truth too," Phil said. This conversation with Phil was as much intriguing as it was frightening. He is a spirit still on a mission.

On the day I was supposed to be on *Coast to Coast* with George Noory, I spoke to my spirit guides, Theodora and Ozzie.

"My friend Gene said, 'we are the aliens.' Does that mean we were transplanted here?" I asked.

"Yes," said Theodora.

"Good ones and bad ones?" I asked.

"The visiting ones, some good, some bad," said Theodora as Ozzie nodded in agreement, always the strong, silent type.

"Reptilians in my dreams?" I asked.

"Intrusion, but you have protectors. Put up protection each night," she said. I felt it, the protection, thanks to Ozzie and Theodora. She is almost pure light, angelic with wings, and Ozzie is the strongman, who looks like a stern, noble, Native American warrior in profile. They make me feel safe.

"The quantum world is the paranormal world?" I asked.

"Yes, that is correct. Be yourself tonight," said Theodora. I thought, who else could I be? The interview with George Noory went well, and I was contacted by many people. Success.

On Halloween night 2018, I fell asleep and woke up just before midnight. I had a powerful vision of a short man in a trench coat standing on the street below our house. I thought I recognized him as Willy, a native Alaskan man from my story "Willy" in my first *Timeless* book. I smiled and waved at him. No reaction at first, then he gave me a scary scowling look. Oh no, that wasn't Willy. It was hard to tell exactly who he was because it was dark, and the streetlight was too far away from him to provide any detail. I immediately got a terrible chill. Who was that? Then the vision was over. A few days later, at around four o'clock in the morning, I had another eerie experience. As I was sitting at my writing desk, I heard our scary Halloween door knocker Ginger had put on our front door sound off. When disturbed, the device says something in a scary voice. I got up immediately to investigate. The knocker is very sensitive, and it only goes off when you touch it or the door. There was no one at the door, but I saw that the motion light was on. I stood there until the light went off again. Someone or something had been at our door at 4 am. No legitimate person would have been at our door at that hour. Not good.

I contacted my spirit, guides Theodora and Ozzie, and asked for their wisdom, protection, and advice. They told me, "it will transpire, belief, and carry on." I wasn't sure what they meant. I tried to listen to my own words to remain solidly between hysteria and complacency. I suppose their advice means that there is no turning back and I must believe in myself. On one of the many radio interviews I was doing, the interviewer asked if I ever thought I was crazy because of all these paranormal experiences. I answered honestly that I had thought about it because my experiences are so unusual, but, I added, "if I am crazy, I'm a very high-functioning crazy…not to brag." But I know that I'm not crazy. We must stay strong and stay in the light, with the light having so many layers of meaning.

On November 6, 2018, I asked my spirit guides if the alien stuff I'm reading about is true? "Yes," Gene added, "remember, it's all true." I continued my line of inquiry.

"Have I been contacted lately?" I asked. "The four o'clock visit, and the little man in the street?" I added quickly.

"Yes. They are watching you," said Theodora. I asked for protection for my family, friends, and me.

"Was I ever abducted?" I asked.

"Contacted, a few times, like 1997. They are interested in your abilities," said Theodora.

"I want to use my abilities for good," I said. All this made me think back to my childhood to look for clues about my interest in outer space. My little buddies in the neighborhood, and I loved to sleep outside under the stars in the summertime and listen to comedy records.

One of my favorite comedians was Jonathan Winters. He was born in Dayton, Ohio (where my eldest son Bjørn lives). His parents divorced when he was seven years old. He once said that they didn't understand him and he didn't understand them. Consequently, he spent lots of time in his room making up characters and talking to himself. He quit high school at age 17 and joined the Marine Corps. He served for two and a half years in the Pacific Theater during World War II. He went to college when he returned and studied cartooning. He started as a radio DJ and then got a big break when he moved to New York, where he perfected his comedy routines. In 1959, Jonathan was sent to the psychiatric hospital for eight months. He was suffering from nervous breakdowns and a bipolar disorder. He often referenced the experience in his routines saying that if he wasn't careful, the authorities would put him back in the "zoo." He was without peer in terms of improvisation. You can see how Robin Williams learned from Winters' style. He once said that "These voices are always screaming to get out. They follow me around pretty much all day and night." He died in 2013 at the age of 87.

Many, many years ago, I heard the late comedian Jonathan Winters doing a comedy routine from his first comedy album *(The Wonderful World of Jonathan Winters)* that came out in 1960. The set up was that Jonathan, portraying a simple farmer, Elwood P. Suggins, was being interviewed by a reporter after having had contact with aliens.

"You've seen over 300 flying saucers, it that right, sir?" asked the reporter.

"Yes, that's very true," said Elmer.

"When did you last see a flying saucer?"

"The last one was last Sunday a week, it was out in a wheat field."

"In a wheat field? Isn't that a little unusual?"

"No, I think they must feed off wheat or something."

"I see, can you describe the saucer to us?"

"Oh, very easily, I've seen over 300 of them. It was about as big as this here room. And when it comes down it give off this really funny whirring sound and the heat it give off was just intense, it was intense. Me and my kid was there and it was fierce."

"I see, and then what happened, Mr. Suggins?"

"Well, then this here door opened up and this little ladder come down and this here teeny man come down the ladder…"

"Wait a minute, Mr. Suggins, when you say teeny, what do you mean by teeny?

"Well, like I say, he come down this here ladder, crossed over the road and reached up and milked my cow like this. I'd call that teeny, wouldn't you?"

"Well, yes I would, Mr. Suggins. Did he speak American, did he speak English?"

"Yes, he did. He had this here glass head on him and there was this little armature inside. 'Hello, I am a Martian. I hope I speak your language. This is a recording.'"

"Then what happened, Mr. Suggins?"

151

"Well, then I waited for the flip side. 'Take me to your leader. Take me to your leader.'"

"Did you take him to your leader?"

"No, I didn't know who my leader was!" This routine was funny, brilliant, and captured the spirit of the times and inspired future comedians like Robin Williams.

The space race with the Russians and an increasing number of UFO reports were in the news in 1960. Popular movies depicting aliens were all the rage. It was in this environment that my interest in outer space and aliens grew. Little did I know that nearly 60 years later, I would have semi-regular contact with an alien of ancient origin, one of my friends would be someone who had been abducted and implanted, and I would recover memories of abduction or being reunited. The Progenitor, Anzar, didn't ask me to take him to my leader, and even if he did, whom could I trust?

Haunted Playground (2018)

I taught my first paranormal personal history course at Citrus College in the Fall of 2018. I was surprised that the administration let me teach such a class; only six accredited colleges in the United States offer a paranormal course. That unique fact makes me proud of our college and somewhat suspicious. Are there supernatural forces at work that would allow this to happen? My students were just as shocked as I was that the course became available. I had 35 incredible students from all walks of life in that first class. I presented some lecture material, we watched some video, we had plenty of discussions, and I arranged for fascinating guest speakers. We also did a few experiments in class, but the most exciting element of the course may have been our adventure in the haunted playground.

I've taught history at Citrus College since August 1998, and there have been rumors circulating about the haunted playground in the old Child Development Center at the college for years. The new center opened in 2001 when Citrus received a million-dollar endowment from Kinko's founder Paul Orfalea. Unfortunately, the childcare center closed down in 2012 due to budget concerns caused by reduced funding from Sacramento. Since its closure, reports coming from many sources have indicated that something weird is going on at the abandoned childcare center. Some of our security guards have heard children laughing in the middle of the night as they walked past the playground on their rounds. Our Paranormal Personal History class put those rumors to the test when we explored the playground.

Toward the end of September 2018, my paranormal class students and I walked over to the playground area behind the old Child Development Center. A few of my students picked up on sadness emanating from the Veterans Center, which uses some of the former childcare office space. We've had two veteran students commit suicide in the time I've worked at the college, and several have attempted or seriously contemplated suicide. Some of my paranormal students had ghost detector apps on their smartphones. I had my electromagnetic field (EMF) detector and my spirit box (multiple band radio frequency receiver). Our ghost detectors picked up on two entities, one spikey and scary, the other a little girl. I picked up some increased EMF readings as well, but nothing on the spirit box. Several of my students said they felt something as well. I walked over to the spikey entity who was by a chair and felt horrible—every hair stood up on my body, and I felt anxiety-ridden, despair, and nervousness. As soon as I walked away, I felt fine. The little girl entity was friendly. She said her name was Melody and she died 56 years ago, at age eight, on the corner. After a while, I told the students it was time to move back to our classroom.

I tried to find some information about the playground area before it was part of the college grounds. The best I could tell, it was farmland. Research into old obituaries proved unsuccessful. There wasn't a girl named Melody listed. I decided that it was time to talk to some of the security guards and find out what they knew about the haunted playground. Dead end. None of them wanted to talk to me. Next, I received an anonymous tip that I should speak to the night custodial staff. A gold mine of information! I was able to interview six night custodians, men, and women, and boy did they have stories to tell me.

The custodians at Citrus work long hours alone at night. It would stand to reason that they would encounter things and entities that we may not notice during the hustle and bustle of the school day. I started by asking them if they had encountered anything unusual at the old Child Development Center. Their supervisor noted that several of the custodians who cleaned the

154

offices and some of the office staff who worked late had experienced odd things, including her. They had reported feeling the presence of entities and heard voices when no one else was there.

Mr. E, a night-shift custodian at Citrus, told me that he had worked there for six years. He reported that many strange things have happened to him while working nights. Mr. E said that in the childcare offices, facing south, through the large windows facing the playground and parking lot, he had a strong feeling that someone was watching him as he worked. He would occasionally catch a glimpse of shadowy figures through those same windows. Mr. E also works in the Earth Science building and claims that it's also haunted. One evening he heard heavy booted footsteps clomping around on the roof, back and forth.

"I was vacuuming, so you know it was loud!" he said. "I would stop and go and investigate, but found nothing," he added. While working in the gym on the east side of campus, he always felt a presence in the upper right-hand corner of the bleacher area. He thinks it is the ghost of a custodian who used to work in the gym and who had died. He also noted that brooms leaning against the wall would often fall to the floor for no reason.

Another night-shift custodian, Mr. D, told me that the campus is definitely haunted. Often, he sees things moving that shouldn't be moving at night. While he was working in the Student Services (SS) building, a giant pot flew off the shelf and crashed to the floor. In the P1 building, objects that he placed on a table moved.

Miss B told me that she worked as a custodian in the Performing Arts (PA) building and the Video Technology (VT) building for 17 years. She would often notice personal human smells (perfumes, colognes, aftershave) whisk by her in the building when no one was around. When she went into the big auditorium (that seats over 1000), she would hear crowd noise, talking, chattering, although no one was there. When she sat in one of the seats to eat her food, quietly, she could feel people brushing past her legs, but, once again, no one was there. Her fellow custodians would run out when this happened. Another time, she was opening the dressing room door to empty the garbage, and there was a red dot on the door, with no possible source that she could see. She decided not to go in.

"Screw the garbage," she said.

One night, one of the security guards brought in a spirit box and recorded human screeching noises from under the stage in the basement.

"One kid did fall down the pit and was severely disfigured and injured by the stage lift," she said. She noted that someone had died in that auditorium of a heart attack. Backstage she once tripped over what felt like a human body, and when she turned on the lights, nothing, living or dead. Doors in the PA building were constantly closing on their own. She once saw a white coat going up one of the aisles in the auditorium, by itself.

One of Miss B's coworkers was lying down and taking a short break in Studio B when suddenly, he couldn't get up. There was something holding him down. When he did finally get up, he saw a black shadowy figure move across the master control recording booth window. Was it Phil Spector? I think not.

"The PA building is not the performing arts building; it's the paranormal activity building!" she said.

Mr. A has worked at Citrus for more than 30 years and is the lead custodian. He told me that his father was a high-ranking Freemason and a famous magician and showman in Mexico. His family owned a circus, and he traveled throughout Latin America and the United States. One night, while he was cleaning in the SS building, the sensor lights that were usually on, went out. He was drying the elevator carpeting with a fan. He decided to take some photos with his phone. When he looked at the images later the next day, he could see a man, a woman, and a little girl sitting at a table near the elevator. They were dressed in old-fashioned clothes, like Quakers, and the photo looked like a negative. Could those ghost people be revenants of farm folk who lived on the land before Citrus College was built?

When working in the old college library, before the recent renovation, Mr. A told me that he could hear heavy furniture moving around on the second floor. Sometimes it sounded like the furniture was being tossed around in anger. A few times, it was so loud and violent that he would call security. By the time the security officers arrived, it was quiet again. He also noted that in the auditorium, the lights go on and off without anyone there and doors would open and close on their own. Mr. A said that he would catch a strong smell of freshly brewed coffee in the back of the theatre even though no one was there. Every time something paranormal happened at the college, he would get chills in both arms, almost like it was a warning. Not that long ago, one of Mr. A's fellow custodians saw Mr. A's doppelganger enter the old administration building even though he was already in the building with another custodian. This same custodian also saw Mr. A's doppelganger when the elevator door suddenly opened on the second floor in the administration building.

Then there is the story of the mischievous custodian named Frank. Mr. A told me that all new custodians would eventually meet Frank. Anyone who works on the east side of campus in the Tech C building will run into him. Frank died years ago, but his spirit still haunts his favorite place on campus, Tech C.

"Yeah, Frank loved working in Tech C, he's still kind of attached," said Mr. A. I couldn't help but smile thinking about this friendly ghost custodian.

"Whenever a new custodian goes to work in Tech C, they always report seeing Frank. It's part of the initiation, I guess. The new guys get scared and tell us they saw a ghost, and we just laugh and tell them, 'hey, it's just Frank.'" I enjoyed hearing these stories from our hardworking custodial staff. They never get recognized for what they do. While we sleep at night, they are busy making sure our schools and workplaces are clean and ready for business the next day. What I learned from speaking to these wonderful people is that it is not just the playground that is haunted—it's the whole campus.

In February 2019, I took my paranormal class to the haunted playground at Citrus again. This time we had psychic-medium Sheena Metal with us. Sheena gave us an excellent guest lecture on protection as it related to dealing with the paranormal and supernatural. She even has a radio program called *Haunted Playground*. How cool is that? After a short break, most of us walked over to the playground area behind the old Child Development Center. Most of my students felt the psychic energy as soon as we moved through the gate. We had a few EMF devices and spirit boxes with us that gave us spiked readings in some areas.

Using an old-fashioned pendulum, Sheena immediately picked up on the little girl we detected last time and something that she described as a male interdimensional being who was hulking around. Sheena said that the little girl had died, but she was a friendly spirit, "a sweetheart," as she said. One of my students said that he knew that a little girl had been run over in the Citrus parking lot where the softball fields are today. This incident happened in the mid-1980s. Another one of my students reported being touched by an entity. I saw a few shadowy figures moving around over by the windows facing the playground. All in all, it was a safe and exciting experience for all, but the questions remain: Who is the little girl? Did she die in the parking lot? And who is this interdimensional being and why was he there? Come to think of it, the young man who was the cause of our shooter-on-campus lockdown in January was captured by the police just 100 yards away from the haunted playground. Coincidence? I believe the time has come for a full paranormal lockdown at Citrus College to get to the bottom of these phenomena.

The Devil in Me (2019)

I was a bit nervous and unsure of myself as Ginger and I waited to board our plane at Los Angeles International Airport (LAX). We were heading east. My psychic-mediumship skills were to be tested on January 26th and 27th, 2019, in Chicago, Illinois. Was I good enough? Would I make a fool of myself? Is all this an illusion? A film producer, I'll call him Irwin (not his real name), had heard one of my radio interviews and wanted to shoot some test footage of me at various haunted locations in Illinois. The single-blind protocol necessitated that we would arrive on-site, and I wouldn't be told what had happened there. He told me very little about each site. For example, he would casually mention that there was confusion here, a lot of sadness or tragedy, or it's rather dark here, etc. Vague as vague could be. The first day I did okay. We visited Garfield Farm and Graveyard, the site of the old Elgin watch factory in Elgin, the Elwood House and Museum in DeKalb, and finally the Tinker Swiss Chalet in Rockford.

All the locations I was taken to were haunted, and Irwin had visited them before with his original psychic-medium eight years earlier. Irwin's TV show idea failed to materialize due to unforeseen circumstances. Now he had revived the idea with me in the driver's seat. I believe our first-day results were not that eye-opening because it took me a while to warm up (both psychically and physically since it was below zero the whole time). I was anxious and uncertain about what I was doing. Irwin and I hadn't worked together, and I'd never done any paranormal investigations before, so my psychic insights were rather modest. We finished the day talking about the results. I could tell Irwin was disappointed.

"I can never be as good as your last guy…he works for the government, top-level stuff," I said.

"Yes, I know. I was spoiled," Irwin said. Somehow, that didn't make me feel better.

"I'll be more relaxed tomorrow," I said.

"Okay, I will give you more time to warm up and not pressure you," he said. Little did I know what other challenges I would face on Sunday.

The next day, around ten o'clock in the am on the 27th, we arrived on location at the corner of West 63rd Street and Wallace Street, on the South Side of Chicago. Not a very nice neighborhood. As songwriter Jim Croce sang in his 1973 number-one hit song:

Well, the South Side of Chicago

Is the baddest part of town

And if you go down there

You better just beware

Of a man named Leroy Brown.

We parked in an Aldi's store parking lot across the street from a US Post Office. The Chicago Transit Authority elevated "L" train tracks crossed just to the south and east. I didn't feel anything at first as I got out and walked around in the bitter subzero cold that froze my cheeks and took my breath away.

"Just walk around and get a feel for this place. When you are ready, I will begin filming," said Irwin.

"I'm mic'd up, so you'll hear me, right?" I asked.

162

"Yeah, just let me know." As I walked around the parking lot and looked across the street at the old post office, I noticed that it might have been a Great Depression-era structure. After a minute or two, I had an image of old Chicago, the late 1800s, Gilded Age, and people walking around in dark clothing, with horses, wagons, and carriages. The streets were bustling with activity of all kinds. A few moments later, in stark contrast, an image came to me of a man standing alone and perfectly still staring at me. He had a bowler hat, a big mustache, and a dark overcoat. His dead eyes creeped me out and gave me chills on top of chills.

"This is a dark place," I said as I walked toward the side alley. I looked across the street at the post office again and specifically at the grassy area to the east separating the post office from the "L" tracks. I felt as if it was connected in some way to the side alley I was on by the Aldi's store. I began to feel sadness and descending darkness. Violent images of people dying horrible deaths came to mind. Torture, pain, death, dismemberment. The side alley was depressing, dingy, with graffiti on the concrete walls.

"This is horrible, this is bad," I said.

I continued to move slowly toward an old lamp post surrounded by an ancient tree that had twisted itself around the post. Trees and rocks, the silent witnesses, always have a story to tell. I pictured children, men, women, all of them underground, trapped, like in a dungeon.

"Irwin, this is a dark, awful place, how could you bring me here?" I asked. The images were beginning to overwhelm me. I noticed that the "L" train trestle over 63rd street was rusted and dilapidated like it could give way at any moment with the passing of the next train. As I stepped closer to the tree, I seemed to slip, but then something pushed me down to the ground violently and drove me down hard like it was trying to bury me under the ground. I felt a sharp pain in my foot and my knee. The blunt force was so quick and strong that I hyperextended my big left toe and left calf muscle. I was being held down by a dark force, a dark entity, and I had trouble getting up. The energy required to do this to me must have been tremendous since I weigh 260 pounds and stand 6'3". I couldn't get my footing; I felt like my left foot and leg were broken. I was dizzy and seemed to be unable to think clearly. An overwhelming feeling of despair gripped me. This feeling of weakness, confusion, and helplessness lasted for a few moments. The snow beneath my feet seemed to be covering slippery cantaloupe-sized round boulders. I struggled to resist the force driving me to the ground and finally regained my senses and rose to my feet with great effort. I kept commenting as this happened and asked for Irwin to hurry up and bring the camera.

As I struggled to my feet in agony, Irwin arrived and began filming.

"You heard all that, right?" I asked.

"Yes," he said. I thought more about what had just happened. Those weren't boulders; they felt like human skulls. He filmed where I had been shoved down in the snow by the tree.

"Were the people men, women, children?" asked Irwin.

"Men, young men, women, and children," I said. Then I started to get this tingling sensation beginning with my feet and passing up through my body all the way to the top of my head.

"There was something terrible here. Murder, death, evil. Great evil," I said.

164

"Okay," he said.

"It was right here, it's slippery, but I was pushed down violently," I said as I pointed to the spot of the attack. I was reluctant to get too close.

"I'm asking my spirit guides to protect me, to protect us, as we try to figure out what this is," I added. I paused to sense more.

"I wonder if this was a house or an apartment building where people lived…a very bad person lived here…I'm feeling, and not from the cold, from the bottom of my spine to the top of my head…that something was very, very bad in here, and very evil and many people killed, in a very brutal way…children, adults, men, women," I said. I began to walk toward the post office.

"I feel bad, this isn't good, this is the worst part, where I got pushed down," I pointed again to the spot. I had never been physically attacked by an entity before. I had been psychically attacked but never physically. I looked at Irwin.

"I don't want to feel that again, I was helpless, pushed down, forced down and under," I said. "You know what the worst part was?" I asked.

"What?" asked Irwin.

"The worst part was that this evil man was fooling people into thinking it was okay," I said. We walked a bit further.

"Do you feel how bad it is, evil?" I asked.

"Yes, in my legs," said Irwin. I looked at the post office and again down the side alley. People were walking by and in and out of the Aldi's blissfully unaware of the great evil in their neighborhood.

"I think I need a break," I said. We began to head to the car, where I did a protection prayer for us and everyone in this neighborhood.

Once we got in the car and drove away, Irwin spoke.

"Notice the people in this neighborhood," he said.

"Yes, poor, African-American, sad, unaware of this," I said. Irwin told me that the location we were at was the site of the Murder Hotel or Murder Castle from the late 1800s. Maybe up to 200 people were tortured, killed, and dismembered here. Dr. H.H. Holmes owned the hotel that was supposed to accommodate guests during the 1893 World's Fair in Chicago.

H.H. Holmes was born Herman Webster Mudgett on May 16, 1861. He may be America's first serial killer. He confessed to 27 murders, only nine were confirmed. He is said to have killed as many as 200, although magazines may have exaggerated that number. The Murder Hotel was a mixed-use building, located about three miles west of the 1893 World's Fair, Columbian Exposition. H.H. Holmes was also a skilled con artist and bigamist. He was convicted of murdering his friend and accomplice Benjamin Pitezel. During the trial, Holmes confessed to many killings. He was executed on May 7, 1896.

Holmes' Murder Castle sat just to the East of the Englewood post office that was built in 1938. This was the post office that I stared at as I decided to walk down the side alley by the Aldi's store. The side alley aligned perfectly with the grassy knoll to the east of the post office. Who knows, there could have been tunnels that extended that far. With that type of evil, just being in the same neighborhood is enough to incur its wrath. Holmes wrote in his confession that "I was born with the devil in me. I could not help the fact that I was a murderer, no more than the poet can help the inspiration to sing—I was born with the

167

'Evil One' standing as my sponsor beside the bed where I was ushered into the world, and he has been with me since."

Holmes often gave contradictory stories about his life, even saying at one time that he was innocent. The Hearst newspapers bought his confession for thousands of dollars. Adding to his sensational criminal confession, Holmes said that his appearance was changing in prison. He claimed that he was beginning to look more like the devil. They say he did not die easily during his execution by hanging. He strangled slowly for 20 minutes, his body twitching uncontrollably until he died. Erik Larsen's book, *The Devil in the White City*, is the best-known and definitive book about Holmes.

When I got back to California, I looked up a photo of that side alley at Aldi's that had been taken in the summertime. I could rotate the picture and see it in all directions. I noticed that there was a sidewalk by that tree where I was attacked, not big rocks as I thought initially, or skulls as I imagined later. I'm convinced that even though I was across the street from the actual site of the Murder Hotel, the dark demonic forces were active in that entire area—these forces were strong enough to hurtle me to the ground, temporarily confuse me, and hold me down. The confusion, despair, and helplessness I felt may have been related to how Holmes' victims felt as they were slowly asphyxiated when he would pump gas into the chambers where they were being held in the dungeon of his Murder Castle. Those demonic forces may be ongoing in another dimension and bled through at the moment I arrived, perhaps attracted by the fact that I can reach the other side through my psychic-mediumship.

H.H. Holmes lured his victims with his good looks and charm, and they trusted him because he was a doctor. Think about it, who imagines that their doctor will torture and kill them? That breach of trust is the worst part. It reminds me of the modus operandi of the more modern-day serial murderer, Ted Bundy. To answer my initial questions about this trip, yes, I was good enough to pick up on the true nature of different locations psychically. More importantly, I was a good enough person to hold my own against demonic forces. I didn't make a fool of myself, but I could no longer fool myself into believing that such malevolence couldn't touch me. And lastly, my experiences proved that the unknown worlds that intersect with ours are not the product of over-active imaginations and illusions—they're all too real. Holmes may continue to murder people in other dimensions, endlessly, with no eternal sanctuary for the hapless victims and no mercy for those in our world who stumble into his evil domain in the South Side of Chicago—the "baddest" part of town.

Tattoo You! (2019)

On my psychic-mediumship test trip to Chicago, Illinois, from January 25 to January 27, 2019, I visited eight different sites in and north of the Windy City. Of those locations, two have impacted me the most. One incident that shook me up was documented in my story "The Devil in Me." The other incident was at Old Town Tatu on the North Side of Chicago. Irwin, the film producer who was testing me, parked right in front of the spooky looking red brick building. I would say it was built in the late 1800s to early 1900s. The front door was ornate wrought iron in a somewhat creepy, Victorian, demonic style. The rounded front entrance archway was guarded by two gargoyle creatures jutting out from the bricks.

"Walk over to the other side of the street and get a better view," said Irwin.

"Okay, will do," I said as I put on my jacket and scarf and knit cap. It was below zero and bundling up wasn't optional. I checked my mic, and I was ready to go.

I took my time crossing the unguarded crosswalk. Drivers in Chicago don't stop. A good tip for anyone visiting the city. Once on the other side of the street, I could see that Old Town Tatu was in a narrow, tall three-story building with a daylight basement level. As I was warming up, I noticed that the spirit of a man was standing in the left-hand window upstairs. The only name I could come up with was John or Jan, but I wasn't sure that was his name. I started to get a bad feeling about the place. All that Irwin told me was that something tragic happened there. That was it, nothing more—thanks a lot, Irwin. I sensed that a man had died in that room, perhaps suicide, but I wasn't sure. There was unhappiness in that building, sadness, despair, depression, and an occult feeling. I also felt that whoever died in that room on the left on the second floor, was known to Irwin.

"You knew him, or someone you knew, knew him," I said to Irwin, who by this time was already filming. I continued to observe and tried to pick up more. A lady walked by, and I had to stop talking; otherwise, she would have thought I was nuts. A hazard of the psychic profession, I guess.

"Maybe some demonic stuff. I get a bad feeling from this place, people have died there, dead people," I said. Irwin suggested that we cross back over and get a closer look.

After we risked our lives again by crossing the busy street, we stood right in front of the creepy iron gate outer door. The tattoo parlor was closed, and the lights were off. As far as we could tell, no one was home. I continued.

"Devil worshiping in here, oh, bad, very bad. I think this is an evil building," I said. I examined the gargoyle creatures. Not good. Then I touched the wrought iron outer door.

"Murder, suicide, people are affected by this place and don't even know why," I said. I looked up to the window above.

"I hear the name Donovan, but I'm not sure who that is. It's not the dead guy, someone else...oh, no, I see a tunnel filled with fire, a fiery tunnel. This is bad, this is evil," I said. I was beginning to get a chill, but not from the cold. This place was giving off bad vibes, and I felt dread and apprehension.

"Illegal activity too, lots of it," I added. Then, suddenly appearing out of the shadows on the other side of the door came a young woman. It was as if she just magically materialized. She opened the inner door and peeked out.

"What the hell are you doing here?" she asked. Irwin and I stood silent for a moment. I was caught off guard, something I hate.

"Filming," I said.

"Filming what?" she said. I had to think of something quick. This girl, probably in her 20s, had long black hair colored with red and yellow to look like flames. Pretty, but hardcore and scary. She had large oblong plugs in her earlobes hanging down and was totally tatted up on her arms and neck.

"I'm a psychic-medium," I said. She hesitated for a moment.

"Oh, okay," she said, as her demeanor changed somewhat.

"But you can't film inside," she added.

"Oh no, we're just outside," I said.

"Okay," she said as she closed the door and locked it and disappeared into the shadows. I was spooked. I had this feeling that she was part of this evil, maybe the devil's concubine.

"She is not a good person," I told Irwin.

"Let's get out of here," I added. We loaded into the car quickly.

I looked back as we drove away. I shook my head—two evil locations in a row.

"Why do you take me to such places?" I asked Irwin.

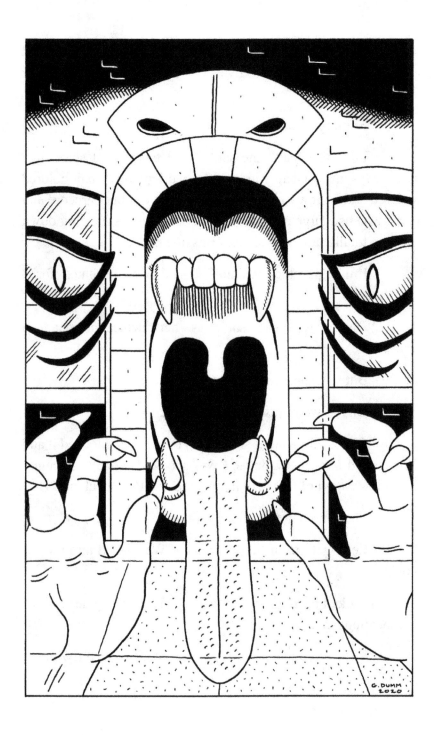

174

"Now I can tell you," he said. Irwin had visited Old Town Tatu before with his first psychic-medium, the super-star government guy whom I will call Hal (not his real name). I was beginning to dislike him. Was it jealousy?

"We were able to get inside and film," said Irwin.

"Really?"

"We had a small crew with us, and the owner showed us around," he said. Irwin told me that two large, scary biker dudes followed them the whole time they were inside. Hal picked up on the demonic stuff as I did. He told Irwin that there was a devil coming out of the wall upstairs. Sure enough, in one of the rooms upstairs, there was a painting of a hideous devil emerging from a hole.

"Do you know what this place was before it was a tattoo parlor?" asked Irwin.

"Not sure, but I bet it was bad," I said.

"A mortuary." That made sense. That was why I saw the tunnel of fire so clearly. They cremated bodies here. No wonder I got the feeling of death and dead people.

"But there is more. The young man you sensed in the upstairs window, he was the original owner of the tattoo parlor, and he died in that room where you saw the spirit," said Irwin. I knew it, and I could tell he was in his 30s. Irwin said that there were scary demonic masks on the walls.

"Was his name John or Jan?" I asked. Irwin didn't remember.

"Did you know him?" I asked.

"One of our crew members knew him, and I knew of him, sure," he said.

The scariest thing was that Hal had picked up on the fact that this previous owner had been murdered, and the two bikers who were shadowing them as they looked through the building were the ones who did it. The supposed friends of the original tattoo parlor owner had him killed so they could take over the business. At one point, the bikers asked Hal if he knew how the owner died. He told them he didn't know, even though he did. Irwin was sure that the bikers would have killed the whole crew had Hal let it slip. Oh my God, what an evil place, guarded by demonic, murderous bikers and a she-devil.

Once I got home to California, I did some research. The building had been a funeral parlor for a long time. The owner previous to the building becoming a tattoo parlor was a man named John A. Klemundt. He may have been the John that I was picking up on during my investigation of the site. Coincidentally, he had died on January 25, 1975. We visited his former funeral parlor on January 27. John had acquired the building in 1922, from someone else who ran a funeral parlor in the 1800s. My sources indicated that it was a high-volume funeral parlor. In 2003, a man named Blackie bought the building and turned it into Odin Tatu. Blackie died of an apparent heart attack in 2006. He died in the upper left-hand room above the tattoo parlor, where I saw the spirit of a younger man. The name was changed to Old Town Tatu by the new owners. Many ghost hunting paranormal shows have visited this tattoo parlor. Many claim it is the most haunted tattoo shop in America. According to one investigator, the wife of the owner of the original funeral home died under suspicious circumstances.

The Klemundt Funeral Parlor was built on the footprint of an older structure that may have also been a funeral home. You can see the foundation of the earlier building in the basement, according to investigators. Rumors are that the garage in the back was a stable and that 30 bodies were buried on the property. I found the current business license for Old Town Tatu and the owner/president is listed as Nate Baileur. There is no trace of anyone with that name in Chicago or anywhere else. I began to suspect that it was a made-up name. One of the many anagrams for Nate Baileur is the very disturbing, "burial eaten." Now, tell me that doesn't send chills down your spine.

After visiting the H.H. Holmes Murder Hotel and then the demonic tattoo parlor, I was tapped out. Those haunting images were hard to shake off. Then I remembered something I learned when I worked in the military prison in West Germany and the maximum-security prison in Minnesota; all the mass murderers that I guarded had satanic tattoos. Perhaps being marked by the Devil had some influence over their murderous behavior and put the person in his service? I don't know, but I do know one thing for certain, my plan to get a tattoo has been put on hold indefinitely.

Lockdown (2019)

"The campus is on lockdown, stay in your classroom, turn off lights, lock doors, remain quiet, stay away from windows and doors." The pre-recorded lockdown message played continuously on our classroom phone/intercom for nearly six hours. It was January 15, 2019, on what would have been Dr. Martin Luther King's 90th birthday. We were facing the potential of extreme violence in the form of an active shooter on campus on the same day that we give thanks for the great works of peace and equality provided by Dr. King. It was dark in our classroom and, even though the voices in our heads were screaming, all of us remained quiet. All that I and 43 of my students knew was that there was a gunman loose somewhere at our quiet little school. For three and one-half hours, we waited in that tension-filled darkness and silence with no information other than gossip and rumors on Twitter or Facebook. We were waiting for death to arrive so we could vanquish it. Four of my student veterans and I stood guard at the door, ready to kill if necessary to defend the other students. I armed myself with a fire extinguisher. Twice someone tried to get in without identifying themselves, and we were ready. It was pretty intense. Luckily the unknown persons walked on. I still don't know who they were.

Since the tragic incident at Columbine in 1999, there have been 85 school shootings and 223 people, including students, teachers, and staff, have been killed. According to a 2018 Pew Research Center survey, 57 percent of teenagers are worried about the possibility of a shooting at their school. I had a premonition that this was going to happen eventually. I'd been teaching college history for 27 years, and each year there have been more and more school shootings. Often on my way to work during the past three decades, I've thought of what I'd do if that

179

day was the day. I was committed to defending my students with my life if necessary. I'm not that special or unique, that is what teachers do; they defend and protect their students. Teachers like Scott Beigel at Marjory Stoneman Douglas High School died protecting his students. How many more will have to die? How many nightmares had I had over the years about being involved in a school shooting? Too many to count. As we waited in the darkness, I prayed that all of us would be safe and the gunman would be brought down swiftly.

On October 21, 2018, I dreamt that I was teaching in a classroom at Citrus when a young man threatened all of us with a pistol and began demanding our valuables. I was trying to think of what to do and by the time he got to me and demanded my wallet, I fumbled, I couldn't see, and I knew I didn't have much money, and certainly didn't want to give it to him. I was ashamed because I wasn't doing anything to stop this gunman. I was paralyzed with fear. After stealing from all of us, he said thank you and then shot the person closest to the door who fell to the floor. I rushed at the gunman, and then he shot at me, but I used a table as a defensive shield and was not hit. He fled our classroom and a few of us ran after him. By the time we got to him, other students and staff had tackled him to the ground. I stood next to him and thought I should kick his gun away and crush his hand. I felt terrible. I felt like a coward. I knew that what was needed was bold, aggressive action because compliance isn't an option. Suddenly, still in the dream, my mom appeared.

"You have to be more present for your family, friends, students, and co-workers," she said. Then I woke up. I think my mom and this dream helped me prepare for January 15, 2019.

When I arrived on campus on January 15, 2019, it was a beautiful quiet morning, even though the sun wasn't shining, some much-needed rain was on the way. The birds sang, and some squirrels we nervously jumping for tree limb to tree limb. Only a few students were around as I made my way quietly to class. Somewhere in a nearby town, a disturbed young African-American student was contemplating his actions that day. He was prepared to call Citrus College and issue a threat. What pain was he going through that caused him to think of this? I don't know. He may have driven to campus and arrived at the same time as me, and maybe we even saw each other. It's odd to think about what may be on the minds of those we pass by every day.

The young man who came to our campus to "shoot it up," as he warned in a phone call, did us all a favor. It was a warning, and I don't think we'll get another one. Now we have to prepare. After the six-hour lockdown and I was reunited with Ginger and spoke to my children on the phone, I felt oddly disconnected. Ginger noticed that I was being quiet and wasn't talking very much about what had happened. I suppose it was also due to the nature of such events; you shut down emotionally to get the job done. I had gone through similar feelings in the army and working in prisons. All that I knew was that I needed to protect my students. That was my mission. There was also this odd sensation of not sensing time passing as we remained in lockdown, almost as if time stood still. I knew we were lucky, but I also thought that perhaps in another dimension, several of us may have died. Another fork in the road of time scenario. After it was all over, I needed time to decompress.

The young student who came to campus to kill us in actuality wanted to be killed by the police, according to law enforcement. Suicide by cop they call it. In another dimension, many people might have died, including me, but not in this one. He was apprehended peacefully by police outside of our student services building. It turned out that he didn't have any weapons with him on campus. During our lockdown, I recruited four of my veteran students to help me secure the classroom and protect our fellow students. We walked around the room in the dark and whispered instructions to the students and assessed any needs they might have. I told the students that when the SWAT team arrives, they will be pointing automatic weapons at us and we will have to put our hands up.

"They won't be like officer friendly, they will be yelling and will act aggressively," I said. The students said they would be ready. The SWAT team arrived after three and a half hours with M4 assault rifles drawn and ordering us to put our hands over our heads. The SWAT commander ordered me to step outside on to the walkway. I had my headcount and roll sheet ready for the SWAT commander, who showed me the photo of the alleged gunman whom I didn't know. After a few minutes, they left and told us to remain locked down.

During the lockdown, many of us had to use the restroom. There was none in our classroom, so we improvised by using a wastebasket and placing it in the back section of the room that was blocked partway by a wall, thereby providing some privacy. We were luckier than other teachers and students who had to use the trashcans in view of others. The SWAT team came back again to check on us about four and a half hours into the lockdown. They were more relaxed, and after they left, so were we. We were finally liberated just before 6 pm.

The next day was another workday. I arrived a little early and noticed how peaceful and quiet it was on campus. Gone were the 100 police officers, bomb disposal vehicles, armored cars, and police helicopters. Just squirrels, birds, and a few students were walking peacefully to class. What a difference a day makes. It made me think again of how lucky we were. What was the next day like on campuses where folks were killed? The same, in one respect, time marches on, the sun still rises, birds still sing, but something has changed. Lives had been lost, and that loss is forever in this world. I once again thought about how lucky we were. It was a wake-up call. What was happening in that other dimension where the young man arrived with a rifle and did kill several people? The next day would be the same, the sun shining, the birds singing, the squirrels scampering from tree to tree, but I wouldn't be there, and my family and friends would be grieving.

Uninvited Guests (2019)

We had a problem at our house. We've lived at our current residence since 2013, but I've noticed, especially this past year since my spiritual reawakening, that there seemed to be extra energy in our home. I would wake up and feel as though entities were roaming around and I would catch glimpses of suspicious shadows. I also felt the bed shaking and my blankets being tugged a few times. My youngest son Leif, who is 19, has often complained of being tired and not being able to sleep enough.

In February 2019, after I returned from my bad experience in Chicago (see "The Devil in Me" and "Tattoo You" stories in this book), my paranormal students noticed a change in me. One of my students, who is a psychic, had to get up and leave the classroom because of the negative energy I was dragging around with me. Many of them recommended that I get a psychic and spiritual cleansing by Esther the shaman who had attended our class the first semester and had returned to give a guest lecture for the second semester. I agreed to go in for cleansing because I figured it couldn't hurt.

I met Esther the shaman at her house and felt safe immediately. Her home was spacious and open and filled with light. Her two small dogs were sweet and affectionate. A traditional shaman trained Esther in Peru. Her sanctuary or ritual room was upstairs, and the first thing I noticed was the large painting of the Archangel Michael on the wall. The ritualized ceremonies took about an hour and a half. During the spiritual cleansing, I saw one of my spirit guides, Ozzie. He appeared in partial profile, his strong chin and chiseled features and deep-set eyes reminded me of a Native American chief. Ozzie exhibited strength and honor and bravery and is certainly nobody to mess with unless you're crazy. He is my protector. After the cleansing,

185

I felt lighter, physically, mentally, and spiritually. In the weeks after, I was able to concentrate and think more clearly. I had no idea how much these entities were weighing me down. Esther said that they were probably attached from my Chicago experience and maybe earlier. Wherever they came from, they were unwelcome hinderances to me, and I'm glad to be free of them now.

On the first day of our spring semester paranormal class, there was another problem. An economics class already occupied the room we were assigned to. I spoke to the instructor, and we both checked our course information assignment sheets, and sure enough, we were double booked in that room. Because that class was a credit class, they could stay, and we had to find another room. Security arrived and helped us find a new room. As it turned out, our temporary room was Pod B near the haunted playground. The room seemed fine, initially, but then a few of my students told me that cabinet doors were opening and shutting in the classroom bathroom and freaking them out. One of my students and I entered the bathroom which was contained in a small kitchenette room with cabinets and a refrigerator. The cabinet doors were no longer opening and closing, but I felt a terrible chill as I entered the room. I gave the students sitting closest to that haunted bathroom area a piece of Palo Santo wood to protect them and the rest of us. We had no more problems.

As for our home, the nighttime paranormal disturbances continued. I knew that Leif had seen entities in the hallway of our house when he was home alone. Leif finally confided in me that in the middle of the night, he was often awakened by his bed shaking and someone tugging at his blankets. Like with me, this has happened increasingly so the past year. After my cleansing, and with Leif staying with his mother for a few days, the entities came after me. Finally, at the beginning of March 2019, this happened again, and then Leif had the sensation of someone or something lying on his back. He woke up in a panic. Everything seemed to be awakening and intensifying. That was it, no more, I had to act. A few days later, I brought in Esther, and she cleansed his room, the master bedroom, and my library office. She noticed that the World War II bayonet that I had on my shelf in the library contained dark energy. I wasn't surprised. My friend Steve who runs a military museum told me that he could tell that my bayonet had killed a lot of people. It had to go. I wrapped the blade in dark plastic and put it in a box in the garage. As a side note, I offered this cursed blade for sale at one of our garage sales and someone bought it even after I warned them twice that it was cursed. Those entities loved Leif's room and his energy. Esther believed the entities were earth spirits, or elementals, never having been human. I may have also brought home some entities from Chicago, or from my spirit walks. Regardless, they're all cleared out now thanks to Esther the shaman. We've slept well ever since.

An interesting aside, recently, the neighbors told me that the plateau just above our house where they have a garden, was the site of an ancient Indian encampment. They found Indian artifacts. That may have something to do with the elementals visiting our home. Regardless, following my spiritual cleansing and the cleansing of our home, I've noted that I had more clarity, increased inter-dimensional thinking, increased intelligence, better management of temperament, and even more physical strength. Life is good without our uninvited guests.

UFO (2019)

We are stardust
We are golden
And we've got to get ourselves
Back to the garden

— Joni Mitchell, "Woodstock"

"Two possibilities exist: either we are alone in the Universe or
we are not. Both are equally terrifying."
–Arthur C. Clarke, author of *2001: A Space Odyssey*

I'm naturally very introverted and stuttered terribly as a child. I never imagined that one day, I would be a college professor and speak in front of people for a living and even host a radio program. Life is often miraculous and strange. I've learned to lessen my fear of making a mistake, of being wrong, and even of appearing foolish. I realized that all of us tend to live in fear and that it's fear that holds us down. I tell my students that no matter what job they take or field they go into, being able to communicate in writing and orally is essential for success. To be comfortable with speaking to an audience, you must be comfortable with yourself. One trick that I've learned about public speaking is to get to know your audience and establish intimacy with them. I try to imagine the audience as one person instead of many people. You must be yourself, be truthful, be humble, and find the light as well as the dark. The key is to develop a sympathetic connection.

To be a competent writer, you must read a lot, and then you must write a lot. Confidence in your written words will eventually become confidence in your spoken words. Our voices must be heard, both written and spoken, for the two go hand in hand. You might wonder, what does this have to do with UFOs? Dear readers, let me tell you, if you decide to publicly announce that you've seen UFOs and have been abducted, you must be prepared for a wide array of reactions from other people and must have confidence in what you are writing and saying. In other words, be prepared, because there is no going back.

My interest in UFOs and aliens goes way back to the early 1960s. Astronaut John Glenn was the first American to orbit the Earth in a spacecraft in February 1962. My mom bought me a John Glenn lunch box, which I carried proudly to school every day. In addition to episodes of *Outer Limits* and *The Twilight Zone,* on Saturday afternoons, I would watch science fiction movies about the paranormal, aliens, spaceships, and monsters. I couldn't get enough: *The Day the Earth Stood Still* (1951), *It Came From Outer Space* (1953), *The War of the Worlds* (1953), *The Incredible Shrinking Man* (1957) and later, *The Time Machine* (1960), *The Man with the X-Ray Eyes* (1963), and of course *Planet of the Apes* (1968) and *2001: A Space Odyssey* (1968). In the early 1970s, I watched the British TV show *UFO*. These films and TV shows helped fuel my already active imagination and further opened my perception of the high strangeness in the universe.

My friend Terry Lovelace has been abducted by aliens and implanted. He wrote of these experiences in his best-selling book *Incident at Devil's Den*. Those aliens did not seem very friendly. Since his book came out early in 2018, he has been plagued by UFOs and helicopters over his house in a Dallas suburb. Terry has shown me photos of these helicopters accompanied by different types of UFOs. On February 6, 2019, I decided to ask Anzar about these events.

"Was I correct in saying that the helicopters near Terry's house are watching him and that the UFOs he photographed were alien spacecraft?

"Yes."

"So, they're monitoring him?"

"Yes." This confirmation chilled me as I thought of the enormity of the paradigm shift in understanding that we're all undergoing.

"Anything else you can tell me to help prepare?" I asked.

"Train yourself. Be patient with the hard work of training. Provide protection," Anzar said. I assumed he meant remote viewing (RV) because he had recommended that training before. I then remembered a dream vision that I had the night before and decided to ask Anzar.

"Was the vision of the candlelight in a dark wind of significance?"

"Yes, symbolic of what is going on. You have to protect the light too."

Big responsibilities have fallen into my lap.

On March 12, 2019, I sought answers from Anzar again.

"The helicopters and UFOs around Terry's house, government and alien, respectively, what's their purpose?" I asked.

"Observation," said Anzar.

"Couldn't they observe him without being so visible?" I asked.

"They want him to know he is being observed."

"Intimidation?"

"Yes."

"What should he do? Continue to speak and write?"

"Yes, and so should you." The phrase "stay in the light," came to mind. It has so many variations of meaning.

Until recently, I hadn't seen a UFO, as far as I know, since 1978. On March 14, 2019, it was a cool, clear evening when I walked outside our front door to look at the sky, something I try to do as often as I can. At about 9 pm, in the southern sky at about 60 degrees above the horizon, I saw an oddly bright light. It wasn't the planet Venus, and it wasn't a star. It was moving erratically, so I knew it was not an airplane or a satellite. It was too high to be an airplane; I would estimate 60,000 feet. I ran inside to get my youngest son, Leif. We both witnessed this UFO. He said the same thing I said—it can't be a plane or a satellite because of the way it was moving. Then we noticed that little darts of light would quickly shoot off from the UFO at lightning speed. Leif saw a green beam of light come from it as well. My film of the event was shaky, and it was hard to distinguish the camera movements from the motion of the UFO. It pulsated and had a peculiar shape I would describe as a diamond. That was Leif's first UFO.

The next day I reported the UFO to MUFON (the Mutual UFO Network), and they included it in their UFO tracking map. I asked Leif if he told his friends.

"No, Dad, they'll think I'm crazy," he said. On my meditative spirit walk, I asked my ancient alien cosmic advisor Anzar if he could confirm that what we saw was a UFO.

"Yes, absolutely," he said.

192

"Who was it?" I asked.

Silence.

"Anzar? What alien group?"

Silence.

"Oh, you're not saying. That's interesting," I said. "Were the aliens here to help?" I asked.

"Yes, they are here to help," he said.

"What were the fast-moving things coming from it?"

"Other spacecraft."

"What about the green beam of light?"

"Healing and protection."

"Ah, so, they are here to try to help with the calamities you told me about before?"

"Yes." That was the end of the communication. I had a feeling that Anzar was pre-occupied with something.

On March 27, 2019, I asked Anzar about the March 14th UFO sighting.

"On March 14th, we saw a UFO. I know it was a UFO. Who was it? Arcturians? Was it you?" I asked.

"Yes and no," said Anzar. Although it was an answer, it wasn't totally clear.

"Were they here to help and guide us?"

"Yes."

"What other information can you give me?"

"Calamities will be lessened. Some will still occur," said Anzar.

On May 2, 2019, after hearing from Terry that the harassment was continuing, I queried Anzar again.

"What is going on with my friend Terry Lovelace in Dallas, more helicopters, UFOs around his house?" I asked.

"He is being monitored, some friendly, some not, some are government types. Combination. You too, you are being monitored," said Anzar. I wasn't surprised by this answer based on what had happened since late last year when I reconnected with Anzar and met my scientist friend Dr. Edwin M. Young and learned more about aliens and UFOs, but it was an ominous confirmation, nonetheless.

I spoke to Anzar again on June 3, 2019. Terry was still reporting UFOs near his home and was in the process of selling his house and moving.

"What is going on now with Terry Lovelace, helicopters, UFOs?" I asked.

"He is being observed and harassed, government and ETs," said Anzar. I thought to myself, why won't they leave him alone? But then, having just attended the UFO conference in Indian Wells, California, called Contact in the Desert, I had another question for Anzar.

"Is it true what I heard Linda Moulton Howe talking about? A secret Antarctic base?

"Yes. Do you remember George?" said Anzar. It was an obscure reference, and at first, I thought of the host of *Coast to Coast AM*, George Noory. Then, Anzar showed me a glimpse of me at the controls of my training helicopter in 1983.

195

"Yes, I remember George, that's what we called the governor on our throttle in the TH-55 helicopter," I said.

"That is what the good aliens are doing to keep the pace of disclosure measured," he said.

"Not too fast so that we burn the engine, I get it. And to keep us going and keep the engine from stalling, which is what the bad guys want," I said.

"Yes."

"What more should I be doing?" I asked.

"Keep exploring, dig deeper, make connections, build bridges, be prepared, the time is coming," said Anzar. I sensed the urgency.

On Sunday, June 23, 2019, Leif and I saw another UFO. Interestingly, on my meditative spirit walk earlier that morning, I had asked to see another UFO.

"Anzar, I would like to see some more UFOs, where Ginger could witness it too. I would also like Ginger to see you," I asked. Later in the evening, I was on my way home after picking up Leif from his mother. We were heading west on Interstate 10 near the Highway 57 on-ramp around 8 pm. There was still quite a bit of light. Almost due west, at about 45 degrees up from the horizon, we saw a bright shining orb. It was not moving but blinked out a few times before it remained on for about 20 seconds. This UFO was roughly half the size of the moon, and I would say it was at an altitude of 1500 feet. It then disappeared. I looked for evidence of an airplane or anything that might have caused this light, but there was not anything in the sky when it vanished. The next day on my spirit walk, I asked about the UFO sighting the night before.

"Was it an ET craft?" I asked.

"Yes," said Anzar. I was glad that I got confirmation and that Leif had also witnessed the UFO (his second). Too bad Ginger wasn't with us. So many unanswered questions remained.

A poll by Rasmussen released in 2019 showed that 61 percent of Americans believe that there is intelligent life on other planets. Only 11 percent of the people surveyed had seen a UFO. Over 60 percent of Americans do not think that UFOs represent a national security threat despite lots of news coverage this year about UFO encounters by US Navy pilots. A YouGov poll found that 54 percent of Americans believe that the US government is hiding information about UFOs. It is unclear what would happen if a US president would suddenly announce that aliens are visiting us. Sadly, it might create some panic, but would probably be quickly bumped from the news cycle by the latest exploits of the Kardashians.

It's my opinion that UFOs and aliens are here, and they have been for a long time. I base this opinion on my research and my personal experiences. I have been abducted, or reunited as I prefer to say, four times: 1964, 1973, 1977, and 1978. Although frightening at the time, I don't see these events in a negative way now; in fact, some were life-saving experiences. I suspect that the circumstances surrounding the 1964 reunion may have been tied to my stuttering which began about the same time, at age six. The reunion, however transformational, was hard for me to process. I had to attend speech therapy for a few years in elementary school. I've overcome my disability and turned it into an asset—I tend to choose my words carefully and I'm grateful for my ability to speak and write as communication is my forte.

The disclosure or big reveal is already in motion. Increasingly, I'm wondering why the aliens are here. My spirit guides have told me that it could be for many reasons. Perhaps we can begin by asking ourselves why we explore strange lands?

Could they be conquistadors? Scientists? Missionaries? Entrepreneurs? Future human anthropologists checking on us with their time machines? Tourists? Or maybe they are our distant alien relatives who have come to visit and see how we're doing and are trying to help us survive? Maybe all these reasons and more? No one knows for sure, which could be a scary thing, but I know we will be okay, and I'm not afraid. If the aliens were all malevolent, we would be gone already, and I wouldn't be writing this book. In any event, I'll keep doing what I do, speaking and writing about the paranormal, UFOs, and aliens, and fearlessly pursuing the truth.

One of my immediate concerns is more conventional. I'm hoping that my wife Ginger will soon witness a UFO with me so that whatever tiny lingering doubt she might have about my sanity can be expunged. I want to share this adventure with her as we re-discover who we are and reunite with our long-lost ancestors and work together to preserve our precious planet before our inevitable return home to the stardust of which we're all made.

Via De Anzar (2019)

I met Lucinda Morel a few months ago at my first CERO meeting, and I had a special connection with her from the moment I saw her. I had the feeling that we had met before. Lucinda is a very skilled psychic-medium, shamanic practitioner, and an experiencer. At a CERO (Close Encounter Research Organization) meeting in August 2019, I decided to tell the assembled group of 25 people that I had brought a special guest with me that afternoon. I said little else and offered no other clues as to the special guest's identity. At the end of the meeting, one of our members said that she saw two people, a man and a woman. They were likely my spirit guides Theodora and Ozzie. That was cool. But she didn't see who I had invited as my special guest—Anzar, my ancient alien mystic advisor. As I was packing my things, Lucinda approached me.

"I have to tell you something. I know Anzar," she said. I was shocked.

"Wow, that's cool," I said.

"Does he look like a kachina?" she asked.

"Yes, kind of, he has a protohuman face." Lucinda then showed me her driver's license. She lived on Via De Anzar. I couldn't believe it. This was quite a startling synchronicity.

"So, you see him too?" I asked.

"Yes!" she said.

"We need to talk some more about this," I said.

"Sure," she said. We didn't have time to talk more as everyone was leaving, and frankly, I was a bit in shock. Anzar had first appeared to me in 1964, then again in 1997, and when I had asked Anzar previously if he spoke to anyone else besides me, he said he hadn't.

In an email later, Lucinda responded to a few of my questions. She told me that "we're all moving into a new time/energy field that will require an adjustment by everyone. Some people aren't taking well to the adjustment." She believes that I am Anzar, and he is me. Mind-blowing! That thought had never occurred to me. She went on to say that "we're one consciousness split into different dimensional timelines but sharing a similar energy signature." This is why I can always find Anzar and talk to him. She feels that I need to make the adjustment to this changing time/energy field and integrate with Anzar to be able to fulfill my purpose. Lucinda felt that Anzar appeared to her to help me make the adjustment. We spoke on the phone a few days later and she elaborated on what she meant by adjustment. She then mentioned that this might involve integration. It took a few days for all of this to sink in.

Not long after the email message I received from Lucinda and our phone call, I took a spirit walk and connected with Anzar.

"Are we one and the same?" I asked.

"We are related," said Anzar.

"Aren't you related to everyone on Earth, as the Progenitor?"

"Specifically, to you. A gift of sight and the connection."

"Thank you. Integration might not be something I want to do. What does that mean?"

"One with the ancestors." I paused for a moment in my walk.

"Does that mean I leave this life?"

200

"Not necessarily." I wasn't totally reassured.

"I have a lot I have to do now for my family, but I'm willing to consider this, as long as everyone here is okay and taken care of," I said. I continued my walk for a bit without talking but thinking loudly. Then, Anzar added more.

"Temporal distortion, propulsion, time travel, it is really simple, distort time, move like a snowplow in every direction," he said. Immediately upon my return home, I started to research temporal distortion. It makes sense, that is how you can travel great distances in a short amount of time.

A few days later, I spoke to Anzar again.

"Anzar, could you enlighten me some more about what Lucinda wrote? Am I supposed to do this integration?" I asked.

"If you can," he said.

"So many people depend on me...I can't risk checking out early. I would have to be assured that that wouldn't happen."

"Yes."

"So, you can assure me that I can continue to live in this life so I can take care of my family and friends?"

"Yes." He didn't elaborate much on his answers. I was somewhat reassured but wanted more. I spoke to Lucinda on the phone and shared with her what Anzar had told me.

"You'll still be a complete autonomous being," she said.

"Oh, that's good," I said.

202

"Integration is just a change in vibration, where he can connect with you more completely, but I've always been hesitant to do that," she said. Lucinda made it clear that it's not advisable for people to integrate with another consciousness without "extreme personal consideration." In my case, it was okay because of the long-time connection I've had with Anzar and because he is a benevolent consciousness.

"I understand."

"Remember, even though I see him, he is for you, I'm just helping you," she said.

"Thank you. I really appreciate your help."

"You know…Via De Anzar, my street, means 'the way to Anzar,'" and then she laughed.

"An amazing synchronicity," I said. I now had some much-needed validation. This wasn't just some coincidence.

A September to Remember (2019)

In September 2019, I was offered an invitation to speak at the Contact in the Desert (CITD) conference to be held in Indian Wells, California, at the end of May 2020. Quite an honor. I owe this invitation to my friends Yvonne Smith and Terry Lovelace, both of whom are legendary and well respected in the UFOlogy community. Immediately, I had to decide on the topics for my lecture and my workshop. In preparation for just such an occasion, I had been kicking around the idea of doing a survey of the members of CERO (Close Encounters Research Organization). After having a shocking alien contact experience on September 8, 2019, and another one on September 22, 2019 (more on those incidents later), I decided that the survey should ask about post-traumatic stress disorder (PTSD) symptoms related to alien abduction. Even though I'm not a psychologist, I've invested over 25 years into researching PTSD among veterans and in 2005 creating a veterans program and in 2007 co-founded a transition course for returning veterans at Citrus College. My brother served in Vietnam and has PTSD, and I've lost friends to suicide who suffered from PTSD. I'm a disabled veteran who also has PTSD in addition to other conditions related to my six years of active duty military service. Suffice it to say; it's an issue that is close to my heart.

My CITD workshop presentation is called: "We Are Messengers: Contact & Alien Abductions While Coping with PTSD." The workshop will help experiencers better understand the abduction experience and the important role the abductee will play in future disclosure. The messages that experiencers are receiving correlate with one another, and are clear: take care of the environment, prevent the use of weapons of mass destruction, and more. Few people in government have been listening—much less concerned—about the health and welfare of the human messengers, the abductees, many of whom have post-traumatic stress disorder (PTSD). In the workshop, I'll share data from abductees who have taken a modified Veteran's Administration PTSD checklist survey. In addition to analyzing the data and explaining the nature of PTSD, I'll also discuss coping skills and strategies for abductees and their loved ones. I believe that abductees have a vital mission and will play a critical role in helping save humanity and the planet after full disclosure.

To further legitimize the study, I decided to model my survey after the Veteran Administration's (VA) PCL-5 (PTSD checklist) questionnaire. The VA's PCL-5 is derived from the DSM-5 or Diagnostic and Statistical Manual of Mental Disorders written by the American Psychiatric Association. First, what is PTSD? The condition known as PTSD can develop from exposure to actual or threatened death, serious injury, or sexual violation. The trauma exposure can come from:

1. Direct experience of the traumatic event;

2. witnessing the traumatic event in person;

3. learning that the traumatic event occurred to a close family member or close friend (with the actual or threatened death being either violent or accidental);

4. or direct experience of repeated or extreme exposure to aversive details of the traumatic event (not through media, pictures, television, or movies unless work-related).

The traumatic exposure causes clinically significant distress or impairment in the individual's social interactions, capacity to work, or other important areas of functioning. It's not caused by another medical condition, medication, drugs, or alcohol. Being abducted and experimented on by aliens qualifies as traumatic exposure. I used the same twenty questions as the VA survey, only changing the source of trauma to abduction instead of traumatic military service. The information I got from this survey was enlightening. I found that more than 54 percent of the people surveyed scored high enough on the VA inspired survey to be classified as likely having PTSD. Furthermore, 46 percent of the respondents warranted a provisional PTSD diagnosis based on certain VA criterion. Men tended to have signs of PTSD more so than women, and younger people more so than older people.

For my main lecture topic at Contact in the Desert, I decided to talk about oral history and the UFO and abduction phenomena. The title of the presentation is "Anzar's Answers: How a Former Fulbright Professor Came to Channel an Ancient Alien Mystic." The official Department of Homeland Security (DHS) motto is, "If you see something, say something." It's a registered trademark in fact. September 25 is "National See Something Say Something Awareness Day." Despite this emphasis and although oral history is a basic building block in the writing and understanding of our history (considered a primary source), the personal experiences of alien abduction and sightings of UFOs are often discounted, disregarded as merely anecdotal, ignored, or laughed at by many in the general public guided by professional debunkers, the media, and the government. It is no wonder then that such incidents are under-reported.

In the words of the DHS: "Across the country, in our communities, we share everyday moments with our neighbors, family, coworkers, and friends. We go to work or school, the grocery store, or the gas station. It's easy to overlook these routine moments, but as you're going about your day, if you see something that doesn't seem quite right, say something. By being alert and reporting suspicious activity to your local law enforcement, you can protect your family, neighbors, and community." That is, of course, unless it's a UFO because then you're just plain nuts. It's a very old trick: attack the messenger, not the message. It makes you wonder even after the US Navy disclosures of what they termed unidentified aerial phenomena, why is the government so reluctant to give us the whole story. Recently, National Security Agency whistleblower and federal fugitive Edward Snowden was interviewed on the Joe Rogan show. He said that he never saw any evidence of UFOs and aliens during his tenure at the NSA. Seeing as how he is safely nestled in with the Russians right now, you must wonder what type of game are they playing? It could also be that he didn't have access to all our secrets. It reminds me of when I started driving a car. You must train yourself to look far out ahead when you are driving, or you will over steer and end up in the ditch. Likewise, we need to look far down the road and not right in front of our noses to decipher the truth.

Now, as for my September to remember and the odd incidents that occurred, let's begin. On October 12, 2019, I had another hypnotherapy session with Yvonne Smith. She asked me to go back to September 8, 2019 and describe what I was doing as I prepared to go to sleep. Yvonne reminded me to be aware of my body as it retained memories. I remembered that I was watching a video on my phone that night. It was an interview by Dr. Jeffrey Mishlove from his *New Thinking Allowed* series. He was interviewing Dr. Ed May, a scientist from the Stargate Project (1978-1995). Stargate used government and military remote viewers to gather intelligence information up until it was canceled and declassified in 1995. Dr. May is a materialist who doesn't believe there is anything magical or paranormal about remote viewing or quantum physics. His negativity and closed-mindedness rather upset me as I drifted off to sleep. That night as I was lying down and listening to my video, I heard unusual sounds in the house and the room, but I couldn't see anything unusual. I even stopped the video several times to listen more carefully. Nothing. Because I was so tired, I didn't freak out, but the sounds weren't the normal sounds of the house. I strapped on my CPAP mask and tried just to relax and go to sleep.

I started dreaming about a house that I don't remember ever living in. It was a nice dream at first because my mom was there, and she looked like how I remember her when I was 11 years old, in her 50s. Then, it started to get weird. It seemed like I was a kid, but I was an adult. My mom started to act funny, in a sexual way that doesn't make sense because she was a good mom and would never do anything like that. I felt very uncomfortable. We were in a bathroom in this strange house. I started to think maybe it wasn't my mom, because I was aroused and ashamed at the same time. It looked kind of like my mom, but it wasn't my mom. It was very confusing, and I felt a lot of tension and stress. She took off my shirt as I tried to leave the bathroom. Then, suddenly, she jumped up from the toilet where she was sitting, and I could see it wasn't my mom. I was relieved but that relief soon turned to terror when I saw the entity's true appearance. She was a reptilian alien!

Yvonne could sense my fear and told me everything was going to be okay and that I was safe now and asked me to describe the female reptilian.

"She was a reptilian female, broad scaly face and body, not much of a nose, like reptile slits, eyes were multicolored and kaleidoscopic, broad mouth, with teeth, and she was smiling at me in a sinister way. Her reptilian skin was almost iridescent. She was alluring and horrific at the same time. She got right in my face and scared me. The female reptilian lifted me with very little effort. She was incredibly strong because I'm big and heavy (6 feet 3 inches and 260 pounds). She slammed me against the wall and was face-to-face with me when she started talking," I said.

"What did she say," asked Yvonne.

"She was frightening and attracting me at the same time…" I said

"Can you decipher the communication?" asked Yvonne.

"I think it was sexual in nature, but also a warning; she was angry. She acted like someone who was taking advantage of a weaker person. Not just sexual, it was power," I said.

Yvonne reminded me that I was now safe.

"You do not have any power here, and I can do what I want. If I want to, I can do this thing," said the reptilian female.

"So, you could make out the words?" asked Yvonne.

"They seemed alien to me, but I could make out the intent…it was partly telepathic and partly coming from her mouth. She was smiling, and her eyes were scary…I couldn't close my eyes or look away," I said.

"Is she familiar?" asked Yvonne.

"Familiar? Maybe, before, female, reptilian, it had popped into my vision at night, around Halloween last year, about when I started talking to Terry Lovelace and got more into alien stuff. Yeah, this same face appeared. There was also a scary vision of an entity on the road below our house in our cul-de-sac…could barely see him at first. He had a long overcoat and hat, dark sunglasses. At first, I thought it was somebody I knew, but instead of smiling, he had an angry menacing look. Now that I've thought about it, his face reminded me of hers: broad reptilian, and scaly. I was so startled that I had to get out of bed and check the security of our house. Really frightening, I don't want either of them to come back," I said. I was visibly shaken, and Yvonne knew it.

"It's okay, Bruce, you're safe," she said.

"I don't know what she was doing or meaning to do. Every night I ask for protection in our house. I'm not afraid of ghosts and the like, but with this thing, I am. I think I've got some long history with her and she has a purpose and it's not good," I said.

"What do you think it is," asked Yvonne.

"I'm stirring things up, writing books, speaking at a UFO conference, and playing an active role in the UFO/alien abduction community. Maybe it's my Snarc comic since the reptilians are the bad guys in that story," I said as I thought more deeply about the experience.

"She was warning me about my work. She isn't on my side, she wanted me to know how much power she has. She can be anybody and do anything to me. She wanted me to know how easy it was to handle me. It's really weird that she was making me think she was my mom, shapeshifting, or whatever. I knew she wasn't my mom because I was aroused and that wouldn't happen with my mom…that's sick and twisted. The reptilian female was messing with my mind. I don't want her to come back…I hope and pray every night that she doesn't," I said.

Yvonne was reassuring but could not promise me that she wouldn't return. As she has said many times, there is no way to stop the aliens from contacting or abducting us. They're simply too powerful.

"Later, when I started to draw a picture of the reptilian female, I became sick to my stomach and threw up many times. Oddly, I was perfectly fine later. I have thrown up maybe six times in my entire life, and this was one of those times. Very unusual," I said.

"That would make sense. Anything else?" asked Yvonne.

"No, no encounter since then," I said.

"I want you to take a deep breath...now go to the night after our CERO meeting on September 22nd. You are at home and getting ready for bed," said Yvonne.

"Yeah. It started as a typical night," I said. "I brushed my teeth and lay down in the bed and started my CPAP machine. I felt uneasy, though. Ginger was in her workshop as usual since she is a night owl and doesn't go to bed until after midnight. I didn't watch TV or play with my phone...I was pretty tired. I started to have this weird feeling like something was in the room, but I couldn't see it. I even shined my phone flashlight around to see if I could spot anything unusual. There was nothing," I said.

As I drifted off, I was startled by a bumping of the bed, as if something was moving through the room. I didn't panic, and it was almost as if I was tranquilized or maybe just exhausted. I thought that maybe the elementals were back and annoying us again. That would mean having to call Esther the Peruvian shaman for a house cleansing. But no, this was darker and scarier.

"The past few months, I have felt an increasing sense of dread at night. I would wake up with my eyes wide-open like there was something in the room, but I wouldn't see anything. Twice I had seen strange lights in our room in the middle of the night," I said. I then thought back to September 22nd.

"A couple of times that night, I felt like something was in the room. I would get up and walk the perimeter and check the locks. My usual. Then I would return to the bed and hear strange noises again," I said. My CPAP machine makes a very distinctive sound of air pushing through the hose in a rhythmic pattern. The noise that I was hearing was different. I drifted off again into an uncomfortable and restless sleep. Suddenly, I woke up and couldn't move. I was completely paralyzed.

"I've never felt that before. This was the first time in 61 years. Not only that, but it felt like I was being electrocuted, from the top of head to the tips of my toes, every part of my body charged," I told Yvonne. She must have sensed my anxiety.

"Without feeling any discomfort, be aware of your body, and everything around you, now describe," she said.

"It was almost like I was so energized or charged that I was vibrating and almost levitating out of bed. I had a feeling of beings in the room, by the foot of the bed," I said.

"How many do you see?" she asked.

"Three of them," I said, anticipating her question and talking over her.

"The taller one was in the middle. They were in and out of phase, they were causing this, hard to see them clearly, but I felt them. It was the same weird feeling that I had in the room when I went to bed," I said. I paused for a moment. "I didn't have control of the situation. They were shadowy figures, three of them, and like I said, fading in and out of phase, like ghosts," I added.

"Did you hear any sounds?" Yvonne asked.

"Electrical sound, the sound of electrocution, a transformer sound, like when you drive underneath powerlines with the AM radio. The sound goes through you and causes you to vibrate from the inside out. But I'm not paralyzed when I'm driving," I said. No wonder it freaks me out when I drive under

213

powerlines; there is a connection. "I hated the feeling of being so out of control and unable to move," I said as I remembered the frustration.

"Sense your body, concentrate on the memories of your body. Do you feel anything beneath you?" Yvonne asked.

"I felt so energized, I was just barely above the bed," I said.

"Get a sense of who is there with you," she said.

"Three entities, very frightening, it was like I was dying, my body short-circuiting, and I was thinking how long can I last with this high voltage surging through my body. I panicked, I was helpless, and that only made it worse. I changed my tactics and decided to be calm and used all my will power, not my physical power, to break free and not let this happen. The entities were making me feel like I was helpless, so I stopped struggling physically. It worked. I felt like somebody turned off the power source. I felt heavy in the bed again and took off the CPAP mask," I said.

After the paralysis, I was trying to figure out what in the hell happened. I'm not sure which was more frightening, the shapeshifting reptile lady or the electrocution. I felt like maybe I stopped a possible abduction, or maybe some other thing or force intervened, but the electrical shock stopped when I relaxed and concentrated mentally instead of struggling physically and panicking. It was only then that I could do something. Otherwise, I was helpless and not in control. Whoever was doing this was in and out of phase, in and out of this reality, ghost-like, and not a clear manifestation. They were in the darkness and were non-human entities. I had never had this happen before. After I got up, I walked around and eventually went back to sleep. I didn't hurt afterward. I don't know exactly what happened, but I believe this is how an abduction works.

"I don't want ever to feel that feeling again," I told Yvonne.

"Deep breath," said Yvonne, "go back to the night you saw the lights."

"On July 9th, I saw a large grapefruit-size orb of white light dart across our bedroom diagonally. Then, on October 3rd, I woke up and saw a rectangular light by the wall facing our bed by the TV. The light started up on the ceiling and then shot straight down and disappeared. The TV was not on, and it wasn't the LED light from the cable box because that light is blue," I said. Were these lights a prelude and a confirmation of some type of paranormal and/or alien activity?

The rectangular light was six inches by two inches. The round orb kind of light was grapefruit-size. Something was manifesting in the bedroom. I think the lights have something to do with these two other experiences. I had never noticed lights in the bedroom before. On the night I was paralyzed, Ginger had heard something moving around in the house and the hallway leading to our bedroom. She investigated and found nothing. I had a severe headache that wouldn't go away for more than a week after the September 8th incident.

"There has been a lot of activity in our house lately, and I assume it's tied to these events," I said.

"Anything else you need to bring forward at this time?" Yvonne asked.

"The Snarc comic book may have something to do with it...scenario is that the reptilians are the bad guys; maybe they don't like it. Maybe they're letting me know that?" I said.

"Maybe they want their own comic book?" said Yvonne. I smiled.

"I really feel that these experiences were a warning to me. A reminder that I might think I have control, but I don't. The aliens can do whatever they want to do, a menacing thing or a helpful thing," I said.

"It's rare to encounter reptilians," said Yvonne.

"The bug doctor, the praying mantis or Jerusalem cricket alien, he wasn't as scary, he was just academic, scientific, condescending, and clearly in charge mainly through his intellect," I said.

My final thought about this was a memory of what happened to me in Chicago at the sight of the murder hotel where I encountered the frightful Dr. H.H. Holmes (see "The Devil in Me" in this book). When I was pushed and driven to the ground, I felt equally helpless and almost paralyzed, but it was a lower level current of electricity, but still caused me almost to give up. I overcame that devilish encounter with mental will power as well. Interesting parallels perhaps?

Epilogue: The End of Our Elaborate Plans

This is the end, beautiful friend
This is the end, my only friend, the end
Of our elaborate plans, the end
Of everything that stands, the end
No safety or surprise, the end
I'll never look into your eyes, again
Can you picture what will be, so limitless and free
Desperately in need, of some, stranger's hand
In a desperate land

—The Doors, "The End"

Men plan, God laughs. That is from an old Yiddish proverb. You can't let being a psychic go to your head. Many psychics and remote viewers have reported that even with their great skills and insights, it's often very difficult to gain personal information on yourself. There could be many reasons for that: wishful thinking, delusions, emotional attachments, or it may be a case of not being able to see the forest for the trees. We stand at the leading edge of a profound paradigm shift in understanding our place in the universe and it's becoming ever clearer that things may get worse before they get better. As the old system gives way to the new, institutions and concepts that have guided us for centuries will crumble and be replaced.

I can't help but think of how advanced Gene Roddenberry's thinking was in his conception of the *Star Trek* universe. He introduced tablet computers, tractor beams, tricorders, flip phones, hypo-sprays, replicators, cloaking devices, voice interface computers, Bluetooth headsets, portable memory storage, biometric data tracking, GPS, automatic doors,

217

big-screen displays, real-time universal translators, teleconferencing, and diagnostic beds. Most importantly, *Star Trek* promoted the idea of working together (all races, ethnicities, genders, aliens and humans) to solve problems and go where no man (or human) has gone before. In the episode entitled "Is There in Truth, No Beauty," Spock wears an IDIC medallion to honor a visitor on the Enterprise. IDIC means infinite diversity in infinite cultures and in that episode, Spock further elaborated on its meaning: "The glory of creation is in its infinite diversity and in the ways our differences combine to create meaning and beauty." A beautiful concept that sums up my belief in the good in all of us.

In another original *Star Trek* episode entitled "The City on the Edge of Forever," written by Harlan Ellison, the message becomes even more personal for me. Captain Kirk and Spock enter a time portal to try to find Dr. McCoy, who went mad after an accidental overdose. Going back to New York City in 1930, they have to be careful not to change time, and in so doing, Captain Kirk's love interest named Edith Keeler has to die. When walking with Edith (played by Joan Collins), Kirk tells her that a novelist in 2030 will base his classic work on the phrase, "let me help." Kirk claims that this famous writer believes those three words are more important than "I love you." Keeler asks Kirk where this writer will be from and Kirk points to the sky and tells her that he will be from the far-left star in Orion's belt. This star is Alnitak, also known as Zeta Orionis. Coincidentally, Orion is where my ancient alien mystic Anzar is from. Life imitating art.

On *Star Trek,* there was no concept of money; everyone had what they needed. That alone is an earth-shattering idea at this point in our development. The ancient Mesopotamians introduced the concept of a monetary economy thousands of years ago, so maybe it's time to consider an alternative? As Shakespeare wrote in his play *Julius Caesar*, "The fault, dear

Brutus, is not in our stars, but in ourselves..." We must take action and responsibility to change the world for the better. Since I was a little kid, I've wanted a glass ceiling in my bedroom so I could fall asleep looking at the stars. Why? Because that's where our future, past, and present lie. The final frontier. We need to learn from our contact and reconnect to our ancestors in the cosmos and then fulfill our destiny on this small blue planet.

We have reached the end of our book, my friends. I hope you've enjoyed Gary Dumm's incredible art and the paranormal stories I've shared. This is the third *Timeless* book making it officially a trilogy. Will there be a fourth *Timeless* book? I don't know. As I was thinking about a conclusion, my thoughts drifted back to recess at Lockwood Elementary School in Kenmore, Washington. We had a standard playground with swings, hopscotch, four-square, tetherball, monkey bars, rings, basketball hoops, and even a baseball field. I enjoyed all those activities, but there was another activity that we started on the playground that I'm thinking of now. When I was in the second grade in 1965, we began playing a new game. When the duty teachers (the ladies who supervised our playgrounds) weren't looking, we would divide the kids on the playground in two and have one group gathered at the top of the hill above the playground while the others remained at the bottom. Then, with a great deal of clamor, bravado, and theatricality, we would descend upon the kids at the bottom of the hill and run them over. We called this, simply, War.

The duty teachers would put a stop to this game whenever they saw us massing for attacks, but we all seemed to accept it as part of what we should do at recess. Perhaps the beginning of the war in Vietnam influenced us or maybe the Cold War and threat of nuclear annihilation? Maybe it was the war toys we played with like my Johnny Seven OMA weapon (One-Man Army) that hopped us up on aggression? I'm not sure. Sometime in 1967, we stopped having our duck-and-cover drills, but our game of War went on for a few more years at Lockwood Elementary.

As I wrote in *Timeless Deja Vu*, "I faced most of my fears and tested my courage many times in the military, whether it was working as a prison guard or flying helicopters. As part of the 82nd Airborne Division in the 1980s, we were continually standing at the precipice of war staring into the abyss." The constant threat of war or actual war has been part of my entire life. I grew up with stories of World War II and the German invasion of Norway. My parents lived under Nazi occupation, and my eldest brother died during the war. How can my family and I heal from this? How can our nation heal from war? Where do we go from here?

For many years I've had dreams and premonitions about nuclear war or some type of warfare using unknown weapons, perhaps alien. Just recently, in January 2019, when Ginger and I were in Chicago, I woke up from such a nightmare scenario. In my dream, we were visiting a military base, I'm not sure where it was located, but there was a mountain range in the distance. Ginger was moving ahead of me as we headed outside after touring through some buildings. I lost track of her and started to call her name. My anxiety was rising when, suddenly, I saw a blinding flash in the distance by the mountain range. The flash turned into rainbow-like shock waves that were headed my way.

"Ginger!" I yelled. But she was nowhere to be found. Then a deep rumbling sound hit me, knocking me off my feet and making it impossible for me to stand up. I felt like gravity was lifted. I didn't have time to think about this strange sensation because a series of flashes split the sky by the mountain range and appeared to be coming closer.

"Ginger! Where are you?" I screamed. Nothing. The rainbow-colored shockwaves rolled toward me, followed by the deafening low rumbling sound that shook me to the core and knocked me down again and I couldn't get up. At this point, I woke up from my nightmare. Rainbow gravity bombs? Do they exist in our inventory? I don't know. Perhaps I imagined an alien weapon of some sort.

In 1968, my sister took me to see *Planet of the Apes* at the Kenmore Drive-In. I was terrified by the giant ape scarecrows and the spooky music. I imagined apes taking over the world. Maybe they wouldn't be as war-like as humans? Or perhaps they would be just as war-like, and we would all be enslaved? Those are burning questions, for sure. The scene at the end of the movie, where Taylor, played by Charlton Heston, finds the half-buried Statue of Liberty, was shocking to me and continues to have an impact on me. It frightened me to think that someday the United States would be gone. I had never imagined that before.

Today, we still face nuclear attack and conventional on-going wars—it seems like the new normal. We also must deal with environmental degradation, global warming, the rise of artificial intelligence, and the perils of alien contact. If that wasn't enough, the United States is in decline, just like Great Britain was before we took over as the number one power on Earth after the Second World War. The natural rise and fall of great powers is a reality, a cycle of history that repeats itself. We're witnessing the emergence of a new hegemonic power— China. Someday we'll wake up to a new world order where the number one nation on Earth isn't English-speaking, isn't a democracy, and has a military (with nuclear weapons) to match or surpass our own.

I like to use my mediumship to help people. My good friend Eric lost one of his friends, who was a teacher. He asked me to connect with her and she told me: "Our job in this world is to minimize the suffering of others as we fulfill our destinies." It was a profound connection for me. Not long after, I learned something from one of my psychic advisors here on Earth. She told me that the real power we have resides in our bodies, and the memories are physical as well as mental.

"We can be stronger if we are grounded to the Earth and reaching for the heavens," she said. I thought of the tree symbols the ETs had in their spaceships. The roots of the tree are firmly grounded, and the branches and limbs stretch up to the sky. They know. Now we know. When I take my spirit walks, I try to get into my body memory, not just my mind, and then I can feel the power and the spirit through my heart and gut.

In April 2019, Yvonne Smith, hypnotherapist and president of Close Encounter Research Organization (CERO), asked all the members a series of questions dealing with urgency based on their alien contact. The first question she asked was: *Is the feeling of "urgency" just as strong today?* I told Yvonne that I feel a strong sense of urgency to help people. That is why I'm writing my *Timeless* books, broadcasting my *Timeless Esoterica* radio program, and teaching my Paranormal Personal History course at Citrus College. I even published a comic book called *Snarc*, based on a dream I had in 1982 of a character who is half-human, and half-alien. The idea manifested itself as a comic strip in our student newspaper while I was studying engineering at Montana Tech and was only recently rekindled and finally emerging as a complete comic book in November 2019. Also, because I'm both an experiencer and a psychic medium, I'm not only in communication with my spirit guides (some would say guardian angels), friends and family, and others who have passed on, but also an ancient alien mystic named Anzar. They have all warned me of coming catastrophes and the step-by-step disclosure of an alien presence and contact on Earth. Anzar has told me that we should prepare by having extra food, water, supplies, medicine, and a generator. Other people will need us to be the voice of calm and reason to help them. The catastrophes won't all come at once, but over time, and it has already begun. The disclosure has also begun, drip by drip. Let's remain somewhere solidly in between complacency and panic, maybe best expressed as heightened awareness and concern, or as my spirit guides say—focused calm.

Her second question was: *Has anything changed about what you are "feeling?"* If anything, my feelings have intensified. There are a lot of variables, so exact dates are difficult to pin down, but I believe this process has already begun. My anxiety level is increasing with each passing month. I feel restless when there is no other reason to feel that way since we're safe and secure in terms of job and home and income.

Her third question was: *Do you feel or sense communication from the beings? Recurring dreams, experiences?* I've had paranormal and psychic experiences since I was four years old. These events happened frequently but randomly. Some of those experiences were of alien origin, including contact and being abducted four times (although Anzar calls it reunion not abduction). I've now learned to manage (not necessarily control) my mediumship, turn it on and turn it off. I speak to Anzar during my walking meditation regularly. So, yes, this communication has persisted throughout my life and has been intensifying.

The last question she asked was: *Have you had discussions about these "urgency feelings" with friends and/or family members?* Yes, I have discussed my feelings with friends, family, colleagues, and students. I feel that our mission as contactees is to prepare everyone else. Some of the people I have informed are receptive, and others are dismayed and dismissive. They want exact dates, but that isn't often possible. I feel like the drip, drip, drip effect is kind of like the lobster boiling in a slowly heating pot. Many folks don't realize what is going on because the disclosure and the events are metered. Some of us will be as ready as we possibly can be, and others will probably struggle. Since I was a young boy, I knew this day was coming. We must remember that our future is manifested by the dreams we had as children being turned into reality.

I've spent 30 years studying America's wars. It's often a grim task. I've collected stories from hundreds and hundreds of veterans, and I've read the last letters home and heard the stories of combat veterans who have survivor's guilt and recite the last words of their fallen buddies over and over in their minds. I have over two dozen human stories in my oral history video collection in the Citrus College library. Many of the veterans I recorded are dead, and all my World War II veterans are gone. In April 2009, Norwegian Army Captain Trond Petter Kolset was killed by a suicide bomber West of Mazar-e Sharif in Afghanistan. I often think of all these young people, Americans and allies, who have been killed or maimed in the Global War on Terror since 2001. A line from a poem by Norwegian poet Nordahl Grieg comes to mind.

"The best, the strongest, the pure of heart, swept away by war." We ask our youngest citizens to fight our wars for us, and for that, we should be eternally in their debt. Captain Trond Petter Kolset's final words to his comrades were:

"Well, this is not so bad. Stand ready; there is much needed to be done in this world!" We live in terribly troubled times and now is the time for good people to do good things. God bless all the warriors who have protected us and continue to protect us from evil. And God bless the peacemakers who try to help us all find, as Abraham Lincoln said, "the better angels of our nature." Now, we must all pitch in and use the powers we possess to save our precious planet and our humanity. This battle may come in many different forms.

One of my spirit guides told me: "The unbelievable will happen if you believe it." That is both reassuring and a little frightening. The truth be told, most people don't want to know if the paranormal is real, and the corporate media (or as the late Jim Marrs called it, the Corporate Advertising Delivery System) and the government continue to hide and/or meter the release of information.

Thank you for reading this book. I commend all of you and admire you for your courage. You're the brave souls who are asking questions and stepping forward to try to understand what is going on, and you're not afraid of the truth. Fearlessly, you stand ready to help your fellow beings prepare for what is to come because alleviating fear and suffering is our mission on this Earth and in this existence. As Anzar told me just recently, "what is real is what we do." Physicist David Bohn said that "ultimately, all moments are really one, therefore now is an eternity." We stand on the frontlines of the long journey home, and now is the time to do something. Have no fear, dear readers, we will endure, for we are timeless, after all. Bravo!

ABOUT THE AUTHOR

Bruce Olav Solheim was born on September 3, 1958, in Seattle, Washington, to hard-working Norwegian immigrant parents, Asbjørn and Olaug Solheim. Bruce was the first person in his family to go to college. He served for six years in the US Army as a jail guard and later as a helicopter pilot. He earned his Ph.D. in history from Bowling Green State University in 1993.

Bruce is currently a distinguished professor of history at Citrus College in Glendora, California. He also served as a Fulbright Professor in 2003 at the University of Tromsø in northern Norway.

Bruce founded the Veterans Program at Citrus College and cofounded, with Manuel Martinez and Ginger De Villa-Rose, the Boots to Books transition course—the first college course in the United States designed specifically for recently returned veterans. He has published nine books, one comic book, and has written ten plays, two of which have been produced.

Bruce is married to Ginger, the girl of his dreams, who is a professional helicopter pilot and certified flight instructor. He has been blessed with four wonderful children: Bjørn, Byron, Caitlin, and Leif. He also has two precious grandsons, Liam and Wesley. Bruce, his brother, and his nephew still own the family home in Åse, Norway, two hundred miles above the Arctic Circle.

ABOUT THE ARTIST

Gary Dumm is a life-long Cleveland resident and artist who worked with Harvey Pekar on *American Splendor* since Pekar began self-publishing that comic 42 years ago. He has shown artwork in exhibitions nationally from Cleveland to San Francisco and internationally from Canada to Germany. His cartoons have been shown in *Entertainment Weekly*, the *New York Times*, the *Village Voice* and France's *le Monde* and in *Cleveland Scene, Free Times,* and *Plain Dealer*.

Currently, Gary writes and draws pieces for *Music Makers Rag* (biographies of blues musicians helped by that organization out of North Carolina) and juggles several graphic novel projects. His talented wife, Laura, adds color to his work as required, allowing him to do that much more in black and white. You can learn more about Gary and Laura's art at https://www.dummart.com/.

MORE

Bruce Olav Solheim's Timeless Trinity helps break the "woo-woo taboo" that prevents us from admitting that sometimes our personal experiences reveal a far more complex and nuanced understanding of reality than polite society is ready to admit. Taboos are difficult to break, but dissolving this one is not just a nice idea. It may be our best hope for surviving an increasingly uncertain future because paranormal experiences offer glimpses of our full human potential, and those potentials may well be the difference between thriving and extinction.

Dean Radin, PhD
Chief Scientist, Institute of Noetic Sciences
Distinguished Professor, California Institute of Integral Studies,
Co-Editor-in-Chief, *Explore*

Dr. Bruce Solheim's latest addition to his Timeless trilogy is his most comprehensive work so far, and thus, in my opinion, fills an important niche in the literature offered by gifted psychic experiencers for ones who have grown to the point of honestly seeking The Truth beyond the shadows. His narrations unfold in such a bravely personable and deeply experiential way that, because of their fine attention to detail, provide a level of implied scientific rigor that, as he notes so well, clearly point out the actual normalcy of so-called para-normal experiences, and more importantly, highlight, over and over again, the absolute Oneness between the spirit, alien, and quantum worlds. For those ready to be challenged and enlightened, Bruce extends an open and welcoming hand aboard.

Dr. Edwin M. Young
WisdomOfTheRays.com

231

Dr. Solheim's Timeless Trinity is an achievement worthy of a wide readership. Solheim candidly shares transcripts from hypnotic regression sessions conducted by renowned hypnotherapist Yvonne Smith. His remarkable experiences of lost time, alien abduction, revelation and a startling reunion are just a few of the memories recounted by a man who truly wears many hats. His adventures prompt us to question our own assumptions about a world that for most of us, is hidden behind the veil. His life of mysticism leads him to assert, "We stand on the leading edge of a paradigm shift in understanding our place in the universe." Entertaining, insightful and recommended.

Terry Lovelace
Former Assistant Attorney General
US Air Force (retired)
Author, *Incident at Devil's Den*

Dr. Bruce Solheim is a college professor and a historian of the Vietnam War. I have known him to be a level-headed and grounded individual. So when he chooses to write about such matters as memories of alien abductions generated via hypnotic regression as well as his inner dialogues with an ostensible alien entity, I sit up and take notice. Given the controversy surrounding such claims, he is very brave to write about them at all. My own supposition, as a parapsychologist who has investigated similar cases, is that Dr. Solheim is exploring the fringes of human consciousness, itself, as it interfaces with a larger and ancient realm that we moderns are only just beginning to understand.

Jeffrey Mishlove, PhD
Host and Producer
New Thinking Allowed

The first two *Timeless* books are available on Amazon…

Timeless: A Paranormal Personal History (second edition) and *Timeless Deja Vu: A Paranormal Personal History.*

You can find Dr. Bruce's new comic book *Snarc* at www.snarccomic.com.

Dr. Bruce has his own monthly radio show. *Timeless Esoterica.* The show deals with the paranormal, supernatural, conspiracies, hidden history, and oddities. You can find more information at http://artistfirst.com/drbruce.htm.

Dr. Bruce teaches a Paranormal Personal History course at Citrus College.

Please contact the Citrus College Continuing Education Department: http://citruscollege.edu/ce/Pages/ContactUs.aspx. Our you can contact Dr. Bruce at bootstobooks@gmail.com for more information.

You can learn more about Dr. Bruce and his work at www.bruceolavsolheim.com.

CPSIA information can be obtained
at www.ICGtesting.com
Printed in the USA
LVHW052136160222
711308LV00016B/2255

9 780578 627458